15 Secrets to a Happy Home

15 Secrets to a

Happy Home

How to Give your Family and Friends the Gift of a More Positive and Loving YOU!

Janene Baadsgaard

spring creek
BOOK COMPANY
Provo, Utah

ISBN 978-1-932898-81-1
e. 1

Published by:
Spring Creek Book Company
P.O. Box 50355
Provo, Utah 84605-0355

www.springcreekbooks.com

Cover design © Spring Creek Book Company

Printed in the United States of America
10 9 8 7 6 5 4 3 2 1
Printed on acid-free paper

Library of Congress Cataloging-in-Publication Data

Baadsgaard, Janene Wolsey.
  15 secrets to a happy home : how to give your family and friends the gift of a more positive
and loving you! / Janene Baadsgaard.
    p. cm.
  ISBN 978-1-932898-81-1 (pbk. : alk. paper)
  1. Family--Religious life. 2. Hospitality--Religious aspects--Church of Jesus Christ of
Latter-day Saints. 3. Hospitality--Religious aspects--Mormon Church. 4. Home--Religious
aspects--Church of Jesus Christ of Latter-day Saints. 5. Home--Religious aspects--Mormon
Church. I. Title. II. Title: Fifteen secrets to a happy home.

BX8643.F3B33 2007
248.4--dc22
                              2007027401

To life!

Table of Contents

Introduction

Most of us think of home as the place where we live. I believe each of us creates an inner dwelling that transcends the physicality of where we reside. Home, in one important sense, is who we are. We make a happy home as we make personal choices that create inner joy. Authentic success is the capacity to be happy at home and at peace with our self.

Most of us search for something out there that will finally make us happy. The secret is—happiness can only be found in there. We waste too much time focusing on the difficulties of living alone or the imperfections of those we live with. To have a happy home, at least one happy person has to live there. Since we can't control anyone but our self, it makes sense to look inside for the secrets. No person, place or possession can grant us joy. Experiencing a happy life is a personal choice.

We all have moments when we feel overwhelmed and under qualified by the unexpected twists and turns in our life. Though we can't control fate, but we can control how we respond to difficult circumstances and people. Someone once asked me, "How can I possibly be happy when everybody is always messing up my life?" Challenging circumstances and people don't make life miserable. What makes life miserable is the way we think.

It is possible to make hopefulness a habit and optimism can be learned. Like any other skill, readjusting our thinking and subsequent behavior patterns takes practice. Because trying experiences or people never go away, blaming others or feeling powerless only serves to keep us miserable. No person or event can destroy our hope, peace of mind or capacity to feel joy without our consent. We have everything we need to be happy but often lack awareness, perspective and appreciation. Joy and peace of mind are not fragile commodities forever at the mercy of friends, family and fate. If we want more love and joy in our lives, we have to become more loving and joyful people. It's that simple. It really is. There is no scarcity in the universe, only in our souls.

Hey, I hear you thinking, "Wait a dog-gone minute. It can't be that simple. You don't understand my circumstances and the difficult people I have to deal with every day."

You're right. I don't. I do know that though we have zero control over so many things in this life, we do have control over our thoughts, attitude and behavior. We can choose to be grouchy, bitter and negative, or we can choose to be pleasant, hopeful and positive. The choice is ours.

Many of us have unknowingly picked up negative thinking patterns that keep us from living more joyful lives. We effectively postpone feeling happy until all our problems are solved and all the difficult people in our lives conveniently change or disappear. If we don't have any challenging circumstances or difficult relationships to deal with, we're dead. Nagging problems and difficult people don't go away; they just change into new nagging problems and new difficult people. It's time to quit feeling sorry for ourselves. We can choose to love someone, but we can't force them to love us back. We can choose to be happy, but we can't force others to be happy back.

Too often we yearn for a life that perpetuates the myth that success equals adulation, accumulation or freedom from trials. We buy into the myth that if we marry the perfect spouse, choose the right career, and earn enough money or raise perfect children, we will finally be successful and then we'll be happy. Yet, no matter how hard we try, hard things still happen to everyone. It's time to stop waiting for a perfect life. The truth is that no one has a perfect life—no one. This is it. Our life today is as good as it gets.

We uncover a deeper meaning to life when we understand the difference between worldly and authentic success. Worldly success is all about money, fame and power. Authentic success is about being. Who we are on the inside brings us inner joy and peace of mind. Because everything we feel and do is preceded by a thought, this book is based on the engaging idea that significant personal change is possible only by first changing our thoughts.

What follows are several fun ways to make subtle changes in the way we think and subsequently feel and behave. As you're reading, first determine if an idea presented may be true and worth action. Then decide to experiment with the idea. If necessary, "fake it 'til you make it." If you like the results after your experiment, practice until the new thought or behavior pattern becomes a habit. When these fifteen secrets become who we are, life does not suddenly transform into a smooth heavenly highway, but the journey is a lot more meaningful and a lot more fun.

The greatest gift we have to offer others is a more loving, joyful self. Someone once said that if we want to leave footprints in the sands of time we have to get off our behinds, because nobody can follow a big butt print. In other words, even if we have great desires and dreams, we have to get moving and try something new to discover our true purpose and destiny. Life is to be lived; we have no time to waste.

It's not easy to find happiness inside ourselves but it is impossible to find it anywhere else. So let's not put off living and loving. Life is not one long hard ride to the ultimate destination of heaven. Heaven will be wonderful, but so is life right now. There is more joy and wonder right here in our own lives than we are willing to recognize.

In the first half of this book there are ideas for subtle changes we can choose to make in our thinking process. Then in the last half of the book there are subtle changes we can choose to make in our behavior. After each section in this book, there are ten ideas for ways to practice the idea presented. Because each idea builds on the previous chapter you might want to stop after each section and experiment with that particular concept for a while. On the other hand, you may want to read the whole book to get a good overview of all the ideas then go back and focus on certain concepts.

15 Secrets to a Happy Home comes with a grouchy life back

guarantee. If you are not fully satisfied with this product because you never really experimented with these concepts, you can throw this book in the trash and get your grouchy old life back free of charge and with no questions asked.

Replacing Thoughts

"Let virtue garnish thy
thoughts unceasingly."

D&C 121:45

$\mathscr{S}ecret$ #1

Replace all negative, fearful, unloving thoughts with positive, hopeful, loving thoughts.

So much of how we feel and behave originates with how we think. A keen awareness of what we're thinking about is vital to our happiness. After we are aware of our thoughts, it is important to label them. Because we can only think one thought at a time, we can choose to replace negative, fearful and unloving thoughts with positive, courageous and loving ones. Our minds are incredibly powerful. We actually create our personal reality.

For example, the first time I attended my one and only prenatal class, the instructor told me if I breathed correctly during childbirth—it wouldn't hurt. I believed him. A few days later my husband raced me to the hospital in the middle of the night because I'd sprung a leak. I sloshed up to labor and delivery where I found a nurse who ordered my husband to go back downstairs to check me in. Then she fired questions at me like a drill sergeant.

"Could I sit down, please?" I sheepishly asked.

Only slightly concerned, the nurse raised one eyebrow, told me to lie down then checked me.

"Oh my _____!" she screamed. "I've got to get a doctor!" (Screaming is not a reassuring thing to a woman in labor for the first

3

time. Neither is cursing.) "Don't push!" the nurse yelled excitedly as she dashed out the door. "Don't push!"

Push what? I thought. I don't want to push anything. I don't feel so well.

A few moments later, a sleepy-eyed doctor dragged into the room, checked me and instantly ordered, "Don't push!" He threw on some gloves, skidded to the foot of my bed and lunged toward me just in time to catch. Then my husband arrived, looking vaguely like a man from another planet in a white space suit.

"It's a girl!" the doctor announced.

"Can I push now?" I asked the nurse.

"Push what?" she answered.

Why am I telling you this story? Because this was my first experience with childbirth and I didn't know I'd gone through the most difficult part of labor called transition on my ride to the hospital and that our baby was falling out. I thought I was experiencing the easy stuff and I had hours to go before I got to the hard stuff. The instructor at the prenatal class told me my first labor would be my longest—at least twelve hours. Because I had only attended one childbirth class, I didn't know what was happening to me. My body and emotions were responding to what I thought was happening.

It works the same way in life. How we think about what is happening to us becomes what is happening to us. Thought control doesn't necessarily take away the pain, but it helps us abide in all circumstances with a greater sense of calm. Like my doctor and nurse kept telling me—don't push. We don't have to push or force anything. We just have to be still and know God is in charge.

Scientists have discovered we often respond to a placebo as well as a drug during clinical trials. Why? Because the patient thinks he or she has been given the drug. By the power of his thoughts or expectations, the effect is produced with or without the drug. In effect, our thoughts become our realities. Though we can't control what thought enters our mind, we can control whether or not it stays there. The power to quickly change our thoughts is perhaps the most life-altering power we possess. The commitment to allow only positive, courageous and loving thoughts to remain in our mind takes consistent awareness, practice and determination or we'll fall back into old negative habits.

I once sat in a class where an instructor, who had studied the human brain all his life, told us that when we have a negative, fearful or hateful thought we immediately lose 30 IQ points. Translation: we get instantly dumb. He told us recent studies indicated that negative, fearful and hateful thoughts cause us to operate from the primitive portions of our brain. On the other hand, he told us positive, hopeful and loving thoughts originate from the portion of our brain that allows us to use our higher level thinking and reasoning skills. In other words, when we are having negative, fearful or hateful thoughts we would be wise to replace them quickly before we do something really stupid.

For example, once while I was loading dirty laundry into the washing machine, my husband walked up behind me and said, "Jan, if water starts squirting everywhere, turn this knob." Then he carefully demonstrated where and how to turn off the water. Well, several months later I was at the kitchen sink washing dishes when water suddenly sprayed everywhere. I was startled and scared. I immediately ran over to the washing machine, reached up and turned the knob. Yet when I turned back and looked into the kitchen, water was still squirting everywhere. Because I was scared, I was not using my higher level thinking skills. I told myself to calm down and take deep breath.

Let's see, I thought. *If I can turn off the water with a knob next to the washing machine, maybe there is a knob next to the kitchen sink.*

I walked back into the kitchen, opened the cabinet below the sink and sure enough, there was a knob attached to a pipe down there. I reached inside and turned it. It worked! The water quit squirting. I was so proud of myself.

It also helps to understand the source of negative thoughts. "God hath not given us the spirit of fear; but of power, and of love, and of a sound mind." (2 Tim. 1:7) Thoughts that originate from God build, lift, enlarge, encourage and exalt. Experiment with this concept. Whenever a fearful, negative or hateful thought enters your mind, replace it with a positive, hopeful or loving one. For example: hateful thought, "I'm fat and ugly." Replace with loving thought, "I am a precious son or daughter of God."

Fearful thought, "I can't do that. I'm not smart enough." Replace with hopeful thought, "I can do that. I can work hard and never give up."

Negative thought, "Why don't they like me? There must be something wrong with me." Replace with positive thought, "I am lovable. There are healthy people waiting for my love."

Do you often feel like a failure? Check your thoughts. Thoughts of failure lead to feelings of failure that lead to actions that guarantee failure. Are you usually in a bad mood? Check your thoughts. Our thoughts are the authors of our moods. We choose to be in a good mood or a bad mood. Do you feel connected to other people? Check your thoughts. When we have a hard time connecting with others it may be because we are secretly harboring negative thoughts about them.

The way we think about our life is always more powerful than our actual circumstances. Circumstances don't make us who we are, they reveal who we are. Obsessive worrying gets us in trouble. It is not always all the things that go wrong that drive us crazy; it is obsessively thinking about all the things that go wrong that drives us crazy. For example, one mother told me she was constantly worried and anxious about her troubled children. Then one day it dawned on her that if she could only be as happy as her most unhappy child, she'd have to be sad her whole life. She mentally separated her desire to nurture and love her children and her bad habit of mirroring their bad moods or being depressed about their poor life choices.

The way we think about ourselves also gets us in trouble. What words do we use to describe ourselves? Do we use words like brave, teachable, grateful, optimistic, loving, curious or generous? Or do we use words like pathetic, incompetent, fat, ugly, scared or inept? We can make a life-long commitment to continually weed out negative, fearful and hateful thoughts. Our character will be the final harvest of the way we think.

As we practice controlling our thoughts, we'll gradually create new pathways or connections in our brain. The greater our awareness and commitment, the quicker our minds will go to the positive, courageous or loving thought until we have effectively rewired our brain. That's how we free our mind to operate on a higher plane all the time.

Mentally rehashing all our problems accomplishes only one thing—keeping us stuck. We can literally make ourselves sick by the thoughts we think. What is our response when we are offended, misunderstood, treated unfairly, accused wrongly, passed over, hurt, rejected or abused? The nature of that response will determine the quality of our lives. If we don't like the way we act, we need to go back and take a look at our thoughts.

Fearful thoughts also take all the fun out of living. Even if the worst thing we can imagine happens, we will discover we can survive it. Life goes on and we are capable of much more than we know. There is really nothing to fear but fear. The what-if disease takes a terrible toll on our happiness. My favorite remedy for the what-if disease is horribilization. The rules for horribilization are as follows: First have a fearful thought such as, *I have to give a speech in front of all those people. I know I'm going to bomb.* We usually obsess over that thought until we're ready to pass out. To horribilize you have to go even deeper. You think of what-ifs until the very worst thing happens—death. You horribilize to the death conclusion like this, *What if I give such a bad speech that everyone thinks I'm stupid and they tell my boss and he fires me and then I can't buy groceries, starve and die?* I guarantee that taking a fearful thought to the death conclusion will always make you laugh at yourself. Besides that, life after death will be pretty great so dying isn't actually all that bad when you consider all the perks. A little natural fear is normal; without it we wouldn't need courage. On the other hand, paralyzing fear is and always will be a fatal disease of the heart for it signals the end of faith. Fear and negativity take up so much room in our heart there is no space for anything else.

I used to have preconceived ideas about how events and people in my life were supposed to turn out. I always worried things wouldn't work out the way I wanted. Now I wake up, think positive thoughts, do my best, learn from what happens then leave the rest in God's hands. It is amazing how much better I feel. "Let virtue garnish thy thoughts unceasingly; then shall thy confidence wax strong." (D&C 121: 45) Positive thoughts create positive lives.

PUT IT INTO PRACTICE

PRACTICE: Make a firm commitment to replace all negative, fearful and unloving thoughts with ones that are positive, courageous and loving.

PRACTICE: Regularly post a meaningful quotation in a place you frequent that motivates you to better thoughts.

PRACTICE: Write a letter to someone detailing several admirable qualities you've noticed in them.

PRACTICE: Fill your mind with beauty and enlightenment by reading good books and supporting the local arts.

PRACTICE: Avoid people who are "hataholics," "negaholics," and "fearaholics."

PRACTICE: Force yourself to find something good in every stressful situation.

PRACTICE: Make a list of your positive qualities so you have a handy script to refer to when you have negative thoughts about yourself.

PRACTICE: Do something you've always wanted to do but were too afraid to try.

PRACTICE: Practice the art of horriblization when faced with a fearful thought you can't get rid of.

PRACTICE: Whenever you feel less than, scared, lonely, grouchy or mean go back and see what thought came before that emotion. Change the thought and see if it changes the way you feel.

Divine Help

"Be ye transformed by the
renewing of your mind."

Romans 12:2

Secret #2

Call on help beyond this world.

We find the path to happiness by quickly replacing all negative, fearful or unloving thoughts. We take the first step along the path when we receive instruction and comfort from God. Negative thinking effectively blocks the flow of love and wisdom from our Creator. Prayer allows us to connect with strength and wisdom beyond our own and helps us see reality with greater clarity. If we want more confidence in life, ourselves and others we need to keep a prayer in our hearts all the time. Then God can truly transform us by the renewing, refreshing or recharging of our mind.

When I first became a mother, I often felt overwhelmed and inadequate. I read every book and article I could find about parenting and discovered that experts kept changing their minds and disagreeing with each other. I finally decided to ask the only real expert. I plead with God to teach me how to love my husband and children. Each time I prayed I felt impressed to change my thoughts.

I remember receiving the impression that if I really wanted to help one particular child, I had to let go of all my most personal fears. Those fears didn't consist only of spiders, public speaking and death, but included fear of failure, not being good enough, pretty enough or smart enough, being rejected by those I loved or even that I was unknown to God. As I gradually uncovered and let go of my fears, I watched my little girl let go of hers. As I replaced my negative thoughts with positive ones, I watched my little girl blossom into her true self. Today that same little girl who didn't dare leave the house alone because a grasshopper might jump on her has earned a PhD from a prestigious Ivy League school and travels the world working on archaeological sites, doing research and presenting papers.

Our thoughts and subsequent behavior have the power to bring great hope or harm to our posterity. In the same way we might write a script for a play, we help author our children's thoughts by the way we think. We have no secret or private musings that don't influence us and those we live and associate with. If we take the time to cultivate loving, uplifting thoughts, we become the fertile field for our children's hearts to grow in. We can't control the elements of sun and storm, but we can be their good earth.

Half of all hospital beds are filled with worry warts and hypochondriacs. We need to relax and turn our lives over to God. Obsessive worrying is a bad habit that demonstrates a basic lack of trust in our Creator. We need to remember God is in charge. Like staring at pictures in magic-eye books, we have to be still, focus and then relax before the image appears. When we focus on positive thoughts and learn how to relax, we too will see the magic in our lives that we are missing at first glance.

When I taught writing to college students, I told them to type on the computer with the screen turned off so they couldn't see and criticize what they had written. My students couldn't write well if they were constantly worried about their mistakes. If they focused on expressing themselves in the first draft then worked on grammar and spelling in a later draft, their craftsmanship improved dramatically. We likewise don't live well when we focus on everything we or others are doing wrong all the time. Everyday life is first draft. We can go back and make corrections. We need to let go of our perfectionism, over-anxiety and multitude of fears. Most fears are blown way out of proportion.

For example, when my daughter Amy was three she was mortally afraid of the tiny, black pieces of lint that floated into the bathwater from her tiny toes. She would jump up and scream, pointing at the horrible, dark monsters. I tried reasoning with her, calmly explaining that sock lint was nothing to be afraid of. It didn't work.

My husband walked into the bathroom, observed his screaming daughter then suddenly became exuberant yelling, "Amy, kill it!" He grabbed the nearest powerful weapon—the toilet plunger—and demonstrated to his tiny daughter how to knock the smithereens out of a piece of sock lint mixed with toe sweat. "Now you do it," he said, handing Amy the plunger.

To my surprise Amy quickly modeled her father's behavior. Instantly, a smile marched across her face. She was empowered. Her screaming episodes in the bathtub disappeared. Similarly, the way we think about challenging people and situations in our personal lives can make them seem scarier than they really are. If we ask, God will help us see more clearly so we can do battle with our negative and fearful thoughts before they paralyze us.

When we rely on God for strength we also acquire a new resiliency. When something stressful happens to us we quickly choose to draw on divine strength. God can teach us how to quickly reframe or redefine the difficult situation so that we can see our circumstances with a greater sense of calm and trust in God's love and ultimate plan for our happiness. Our Creator is ever ready to help us. When we have God at our side, nothing is impossible. "If God be for us, who can be against us?" (Romans 8:31)

Our Creator will also help us learn to see other people in a more loving way. To explore this idea, think of someone you do not have kind feelings for. Perhaps you even hate this person and feel righteously justified with your evaluation of their worth. When you're willing to be truly sincere, offer a prayer and ask for help to see that person the way God does. If you continue praying about this person long enough, you will eventually be enlightened. That person may not ever change, but the way you think about that person will change dramatically. You will no longer be self-deceived and will be granted a glimpse into that person's soul. Praying about the people you dislike or hate has the potential to change your life like nothing else.

God will also help us let go of the past. We all have enough bad things happen to use as an excuse to be miserable for the rest of our lives. We can't change the past; even God can't change the past. Yet, with divine help, we can change the hold the past has over us through repentance or forgiveness. Through the Atonement of Jesus Christ, God will help us let go of the past in a way that it will no longer have a negative impact on our thoughts and behavior in the present.

The war in heaven has already been waged and won. Good triumphed over evil. The only battle that remains is the battle for our souls. That battle in waged largely in our minds. ". . . be ye transformed by the renewing of your mind." (Romans 12:2) We have been promised we are never alone to bear our burdens or face our challenges. "Fear not: for they that be with us are more than they that be with them." (2 Kings 6:16) So we can let go of negativity, hate and fear. If we ask God to help us, our hearts will change in ways we never dreamed possible.

PUT IT INTO PRACTICE

PRACTICE: The next time something difficult happens to you, pray. Ask God for help to reframe or redefine your circumstances.

PRACTICE: Stressed-out? Ask yourself: "Have I prayed about this?"

PRACTICE: Take a vow of kindness: volunteer, open doors, say thank you, respect differing opinions, allow strangers to cut in front of you or pick up litter.

PRACTICE: Forgive someone who has harmed you.

PRACTICE: Remember you can talk to God any time, day or night. God is never too busy for you and has all the time you need.

PRACTICE: Write a letter to yourself detailing how you are going to reframe a negative experience in your life in a more positive or hopeful way.

PRACTICE: With God's help, face and overcome one personal fear.

PRACTICE: Write past mistakes on a paper, tape them to a balloon and let them go figuratively and literally.

PRACTICE: Keep a running gratitude prayer in your mind and heart all the time.

PRACTICE: When things don't go as planned or you don't get what you want, ask God for renewed strength and trust in His timing and plan for you.

Attitude
Adjustments

"The Lord did strengthen
them that they could bear up
their burdens with ease, and
they did submit cheerfully
and with patience to all
the will of the Lord."

Mosiah 24:15

Secret #3

If you can't change your circumstances, change your attitude.

Once we replace negative thoughts and call on God, we are better able to become more aware of our attitudes or the way we choose to think about our circumstances.

One day I walked into the room just as one of my young sons punched his little brother in the nose. I immediately began a lecture.

"In our home, we don't hit each other. When we feel mad, we talk about it," I said, placing my hands on my hips.

My young son obviously felt bad about what he'd just done and even worse about getting caught. He lowered his eyebrows and in a frustrated voice asked, "Why did we have to come down from heaven anyway?"

"When you were in heaven you were so excited about coming to earth, you shouted for joy," I answered.

My young son lowered his eyebrows again, squished up his lips and thought for a moment before he replied, "Yeah, well if I did, I was just teasing."

He expressed well what many of us feel like when faced with yet another problem. We wonder, *What was I thinking? I shouted for joy for this?*

Yes! Though life can be difficult, it helps to remember that we actually signed up for mortality with enthusiasm. Everything we experience in this life gives us the opportunity to develop character. The person we become because of our experiences is the only thing we take with us when we die. Since none of us are going to get out of this alive, we might as well make the best of things while we're here. Making the best of all our personal circumstances is the formula for developing a healthy attitude.

Paradoxically heaven didn't have the requisite misery and pain for us to experience a fullness of joy. In heaven we couldn't have children and "would have remained in a state of innocence, having no joy, for (we) knew no misery; doing no good, for (we) knew no sin. But behold, all things have been done in the wisdom of him who knoweth all things. Adam fell that men might be; and men are, that (we) might have joy." (2 Nephi 2:23-25)

Wow! So we're here to experience joy—and we can't experience joy without experiencing misery and pain. That pretty much sums up the point of life. We're here to gain knowledge, understanding, and personal experience through both joy and pain. There are certain character traits we develop only through difficult circumstances, such as patience, wisdom, unselfishness and love. In this life all things have their opposite—good and evil, virtue and vice, light and darkness, pleasure and pain, life and death. We all have difficult experiences to deal with. We have no control over many of the circumstances in our life, but we do have control over the person we become and the character we develop because we have the master controls over our attitude.

One of my favorite stories told to me as a child involves two frogs hopping through the barn one bright and sunny morning. Everything was going well. They were happy and chatting away, but they forgot to watch where they were going. Suddenly both frogs plopped into the vat of cream. One frog looked around him, saw the mess he was in, assessed the probable outcome of the situation and immediately despaired.

Big vat of cream. No way out, the first frog thought to himself. *Why do bad things always happen to me? I've been trying to do what's right. I don't deserve this. Where are you God? You've abandoned me.*

God was right there ready to help, but the first frog forgot to ask. In the end the frog cursed God, drowned and died. Now the second frog also assessed the situation.

Big vat of cream. No way out, the second frog thought. *You know I haven't had my cardiovascular workout yet today. I think I'll try the back stroke.*

The second frog swam around and around the vat of cream humming a tune about his wife and children and how much he loved them. Low and behold, before he knew it, the cream turned into butter—and the frog hopped out.

Both frogs found themselves in the same awful, hopeless situation. Each frog chose a response. All of us are going to find ourselves in various vats of trouble that appear hopeless. Sometimes we just have to hang on or try the back stroke to keep our selves afloat. If we don't give up and keep our covenants with God, everything that happens to us will be for our good—in time.

I once knew a woman named Blanche who was confined to bed for years. While I was in bed because of premature labor, we became telephone buddies. Before bed confinement, Blanche had been confined to a wheelchair for thirty years because of a mistake during surgery. After she returned home from the surgery, her husband left her. Blanche was forced to raise her four children alone in her wheelchair. She had every reason to focus on what she had lost. In fact, she did for a while. She tried to sue the doctor. She was discouraged and disheartened. But one day she told me she looked into the eyes of her daughter and realized everything her child had lost.

Blanche realized her daughter needed a mother who was happy and a mother who had forgiven the doctor and her father. She had every reason to be bitter after everything she had lost. Instead, she decided to focus on what remained. In her later years she became bedridden. Blanche had one window in her bedroom from which she could see a single tree. During our telephone conversations, she would describe in intimate detail the intricate changes the seasons would bring to her tree.

"Its' such a miracle to be able to see," Blanche said. "I have so much to live for."

Blanche used the same detailed descriptions when she spoke of her grandchildren. She saw beauty and blessings everywhere she looked because she chose to see with a grateful heart, even when her entire landscape was limited to a tiny bedroom and she was forced to use a bedpan. If I had been Blanche, I would have been upset that I couldn't walk or get out of bed. But Blanche knew the only true power we possess is our ability to see life as it really is. Life, as it really is, is downright amazing.

Blanche understood the value of creating our own celebrations. She often called me to wish me a happy Tuesday. She didn't wait for holidays or birthdays to celebrate or share her love of life. She understood we have to be in charge of our own joy and create our own celebrations—for life is short. She had determined to respond positively to the events and people in her life she had no control over. Her motto was, "This is the day which the Lord hath made; we will rejoice and be glad in it." (Psalm 118: 24)

We are not responsible for what happens to us—but we are responsible for how we respond to what happens to us. Pain is part of all our lives, but suffering is optional. We can't change the past, but we can change the hold it has over us. We need not be overly concerned with what others do or say. Our character development and personal growth is in our hands. Though we can't always change our difficult circumstances, we can always change our attitude. When we can't change our circumstances, it is time to change our hearts.

PUT IT INTO PRACTICE

PRACTICE: Find one activity you have to do, but hate to do. Then determine to change your attitude about the task. For example, if you hate to do the dishes then consistently fill your mind with all the joys derived from washing dishes. Keep this up until you actually look forward to doing the task you used to hate.

PRACTICE: Face a perplexing relationship or life problem by asking yourself, "Is this something I can change?" If not, change your response.

PRACTICE: Get adequate nutrition, rest, sleep, work, exercise and play everyday.

PRACTICE: Stop all gossiping, back biting and complaining about people behind their backs. If you have a problem with someone, go to them and try to solve it. Never say anything about someone you wouldn't say to their face.

PRACTICE: Attend a baptism. Contemplate starting over.

PRACTICE: Take the sacrament with more reverence and think about what you can do to make changes in yourself to bring more joy and love to your family and friends.

PRACTICE: Stop waiting until things calm down before you get your act together. Make the reality of your life right now as satisfying as you possibly can.

PRACTICE: Don't leave difficult situations until you've learned something new about love.

PRACTICE: Take a close look at yourself when others annoy you.

PRACTICE: Give someone something you always wanted but never received.

Gratitude Graces

"Were there not ten
cleansed? But where
are the nine?"

Luke 17:17

Secret # 4

Be grateful for everything.

After we replace negative thoughts, call on God and change our attitude, we are able to feel more appreciation for what we already have. Gratitude is the best non-prescription antidepressant in the world. I've never met a grateful person who was not happy—or a happy person who was not grateful. Gratitude allows us to enjoy life before things get better. In fact, when we want what we have, we always get what we want. Loss is part of the cycle of life; yet without exception day always follows night and spring always follows winter. When we are grateful for literally everything, we've learned yet another key secret to happiness.

Let me illustrate. One of my favorite folk tales concerns a king who had two sons. One son was ungrateful, grouchy and a regular pain to be around. The other son was grateful, optimistic and a joy to spend time with. One day the king tried an experiment. He gave the ungrateful son a new pony and he gave the grateful son a room full of manure. After an hour passed, the king went to check on his two sons. When he got to the stable, he found his ungrateful son sitting next to the new pony with a scowl.

"Son," the king asked, "why aren't you happy? I just gave you a new pony."

"Now you probably expect me to feed it and clean up after it," the son replied.

Discouraged, the king went to the other room where he found

29

his grateful son eagerly shoveling manure over his shoulder with a big grin on his face.

"Son," the king said, "face reality. You are in a room full of manure."

The grateful son replied, "Oh Father, thank you. With all this manure, there's got to be a pony in here somewhere!"

In the end, the king took the pony away from the ungrateful son and gave it to the grateful son. So, in fact, there was a pony in there somewhere. Being grateful is the best antidote to hopelessness and the ultimate bad attitude correction. Grateful people have just as many difficult circumstances to deal with as ungrateful people. The difference is grateful people choose to count their blessings instead of their problems.

No one likes to be around complainers. When we focus our thoughts on what we're grateful for, we make the best of what life hands us. Gratitude awakens us to the miracles all around us—the road we drive on, warm water for our shower and fresh food to eat in the winter. Even the very air we breathe is an endowment that can be given or taken away at any moment. Each day is a fragile gift to be savored and enjoyed. When we die, we take who we are, what we've learned and our loving relationships. That's it. Why let anything else matter more?

Gratitude isn't just a feeling. When we are truly grateful we share and serve. What are we presently doing with our money, possessions, talents, knowledge and time? Do we hoard all our gifts or do we share them and serve others? What are we presently doing with God's stewardship to us? We actually own nothing. Only what we give away is truly ours to keep. Do we see clearly that authentic wealth includes love, peace of mind, appreciation, inner harmony and fulfilling our divine destiny?

When we focus on being grateful for what we have instead of longing for what we don't have, what we have will always be enough. I remember a time in my life when I had to learn this lesson the hard way. One evening after we moved into our first new home, my husband seeded our front yard dirt with grass seed. The next morning, he told me it was important to keep the dirt wet or the grass seeds wouldn't sprout. Then he kissed me on the cheek and left for work. Since it was the middle of July, this assignment was a full-time job. On top of that, I was pregnant and had two baby daughters to care for. I stood on the front porch, feeling lightheaded and nauseated, squirting the dirt while my one-and two-year-old daughters tumbled down the steps, threw their shoes in the ditch and stuffed rocks up their noses. After days and days of constant watering, our front yard grew the biggest, greenest weeds in the neighborhood.

"This if my life," I remember mumbling as I sprayed the dirt. "I water weeds. I feed one end of my girls and clean up the other. Nothing I do really matters."

A few days later, I had serious complications with my pregnancy and late one night began hemorrhaging. My husband quickly raced me to the emergency room of the nearest hospital. After the doctor arrived and slowed the bleeding, he told us our baby was dead. It broke my heart to leave the hospital that night with empty arms. When we arrived home, I found our two baby daughters asleep on our bed. Now, I'd always loved my daughters, but never quite like I did at that night.

Thank you God, I thought with new awareness. *They are alive. It is such a miracle to have a child who is alive.*

Several days later when I went out to check on our front lawn of weeds, I found something I'll never forget. If I got down on my hands and knees and took out a magnifying glass, I could see tiny blades of grass so small they looked like green sewing thread. All my watering and weeding was starting to pay off. I understood I needed faith and patience during the growing season. It occurred to me that all the work involved in caring for a young family was like our newly seeded lawn—a lot of labor and weeds at first. You can't see the roots setting deep in the rich soil of parental love. Then when the tender seedlings begin to grow, they have the means to sustain them through times of drought and frost. I also realized if I didn't stop and notice the miracles of my everyday life, I would miss the joy in the journey. In time, my children, like the lawn, would not require my constant care—the fleeting moments of childhood will have passed.

Gratitude moves us to share laughter and make loving human connections. Gratitude invites us to feel at peace about our past, gives us the capacity to experience true joy today and allows us to create a hopeful vision for tomorrow. Life isn't easy. Yet once we accept that life is difficult, a series of problems to face and work through, it ceases to be so hard. When we accept life as it is, we are free to embrace it—to live life fully and intimately. Just being alive for one more day is a grand thing.

Ask yourself, "Would I trade my family for a million dollars?" If your answer is no, then you are a millionaire. True wealth is an inner awareness we attain by taking personal inventory of our present assets—health, friends, family, work, food and shelter. If we don't appreciate what we have, more will never be enough. One of the best parts of growing older is that most of those things we wanted and couldn't afford when we were young we no longer want. We learn to relish simplicity. The less we want the more we have. The simpler we make our lives, the more abundant they become. Spending unhurried hours with those you love is priceless.

The joy of life is the journey. This is it. It doesn't get better than this. So we can stop waiting. We can eat more ice-cream, go barefoot, watch more sunsets, laugh more and cry less. Life is to be lived and loved as we go along. Like a roller coaster ride; it's the hills and valleys that make it a thrill. The secret of life is to be grateful for the whole breathtaking ride.

PUT IT INTO PRACTICE

PRACTICE: Truly experience this day's quiet joys and simple pleasures. Savor a simple meal. Relish the love of a child. Take delight in the changing seasons. Smell the lilacs, listen to the sound of waves crashing on the beach, touch a newborn kitten or gaze up at the star-lit sky.

PRACTICE: Make a list some of all the things you're grateful for. Hang it in an obvious place and read it often.

PRACTICE: Write a sincere letter of appreciation to someone once a week, month or year. Be very specific about how they have positively impacted your life.

PRACTICE: Begin a gratitude journal. Find and write down something you are grateful for every day, week or month.

PRACTICE: Volunteer at a hospital or school.

PRACTICE: Say thank you to a family member every day. Going to work, fixing a meal, putting gas in the car and cleaning the bathroom is seldom appreciated.

PRACTICE: When you wake, thank God for the gift of one more splendid day to be alive.

PRACTICE: Create a holy place for yourself where you regularly count your blessings.

PRACTICE: Find a personal way to truly feel God's love for you every single day.

PRACTICE: Give someone a gift because you are grateful for their influence in your life.

Perspective Corrections

"Make a joyful noise unto
the Lord . . . serve the
Lord with gladness: come
before his presence with
singing. Enter into his gates
with thanksgiving . . ."

Psalm 100:1-2,4

Secret #5

Change the way you view your circumstances.

After we replace our negative thoughts, call on God, improve our attitude and feel more gratitude we are better equipped to acquire a more honest perspective about our circumstances. Otherwise we may remain deeply self-deceived.

For example, by the raise of hands, how many of you think you are absolutely, world-class wealthy? Whenever I ask that question, no one ever raises their hand. What if I asked you this question instead: How many of you live in a home with a non-dirt floor? Would you raise your hand? If you would, you should realize that according to the United Nations, you are in the top 50% of the world's wealthiest people based on that response alone. Now what if I asked you this question: How many of you live in a home with a window, a door and more than one room? Would you raise your hand? If you would, you are in the top 20% of the world's wealthiest people. Now what if I asked you this question: How many of you have a pair of shoes, a change of underwear, can choose between two or more foods to eat and can read? If you answer yes, you are in the top 10% of the world's wealthiest people.

Now, I'm going to ask you the first question I posed—again. How many of you think you are absolutely, world-class wealthy? My guess is that all of you would raise your hand now. Why? Did your circumstances change? No. Your perspective changed. We might go through our whole lives thinking we're poor, when we're actually wealthy. If we could be wrong about something like that, what else might we be wrong about?

A limited perspective often traps us in a mistaken diagnosis of self-pity or self-aggrandizement. I remember clearly the day I glanced around me in the pediatrician's office while waiting for my first baby's check-up. The room was full of snot-nosed whiney ill-dressed misbehaving children. None of my children will ever look or act like that, I thought to myself. Two decades later I remember sitting in the pediatrician's office for my last baby's check-up. My son was running around like a maniac with his light saber chasing unsuspecting toddlers. His teenage sister was listening to music through headphones and a bad attitude was oozing out her bared teeth. Another child was picking his nose and my baby was filling her diaper and burping at the same time with so much gusto it made my eyes water. Funny thing—I really didn't care when I noticed a new mother across the room eyeing my brood with a critical eye. Eventually all children teach their parents humility. I just smiled and waved.

Likewise, I used to feel so embarrassed for the older women I saw in public with their makeup applied to the incorrect part of their face. They didn't seem to notice their lipstick was protruding way beyond their actual lip lines or that their mascara was smeared. Now I'm the older woman who hasn't figured out how to apply make-up when I can't see without putting my glasses on. If I put my glasses on, I can't apply my eye makeup because my glasses are in the way. So I take off my glasses and just kind of guess, hoping for the best. I often see young people with 20/20 vision look at me quizzically, but I don't waste a moment in embarrassment. I rather enjoy providing comic relief for the younger generation.

One woman told me she wasted many years feelings sorry for herself and her daughter who was born deaf. After she spent time in the hospital when her child needed surgery, this woman left feeling overwhelmingly blessed. Why? She'd spent the night walking the halls with other parents who had children who were missing brains, eyes, arms and legs. The child in the next room died during the night. Her child's deafness didn't seem so awful any more.

I spoke with a new widow once who taught me to keep a daily perspective of enjoyment and celebration. She and her husband lived frugally for forty years, never going on expensive vacations or buying each other nice gifts. They socked away every spare dime for "retirement." They were really going to start enjoying life—when her husband retired. Well, her husband died unexpectedly the day before he retired. This woman told me if she had it to do over she would enjoy their money and their time together as they went along, not waiting for some dream that never happened.

I wrote a number of books and hundreds of newspaper columns and magazine articles while I was learning how to enjoy motherhood during those early years. I knew the moment I stepped into grandmahood I would have a major paradigm shift. Well, I became a new mother for the tenth time and a grandmother within hours of each other, so I got this interesting view. My perspective instantly eternalized. I was overcome with the magnitude of what it meant to have a child placed in my arms. I knew my choice to love or not love this child would have a huge impact on thousands of lives.

I figured this perspective adjustment was coming because every grandmother I talked with got a glimmer in her eyes whenever I told them about the weird things my children were doing. I didn't think my life was all that wonderful at the time. I certainly didn't appreciate being told to enjoy sleepless nights, potty training, chicken pox marathons, science fair projects, Cub Scout pinewood derbies, proms, driver's license practice sessions and all the other difficult experiences I was going through. What I really wanted was someone to validate how hard it is to be a mother. I think I was also searching for someone to guarantee all my hard work would be worth it and all my children were going to turn out all right.

Now I know that anything in life that is worthwhile is hard work. Now I know that loving a child is always worth it. So, most of my fear and self pity is gone, leaving a lot more room for joy. My life has become less about me and more about others.

Nursing old wounds, obsessing on problems, anticipating the worst, indulging in comparisons, dwelling on the past and second-guessing past choices are all good ways to think if we want to be miserable. This life is just a drop in the sea of eternity. We can drink deep from the well of love. We can uplift, encourage, nurture and inspire. Whenever we're tempted to retreat into small living, we can remember who we are and tell ourselves to start acting like the children of God we are.

Each moment is precious and deserves to be savored. If we had a glimpse into the magnitude of our influence, we wouldn't live one more day without offering our love. Life is a glorious thing no matter what our present circumstances may be. For all experience is like the entrance or archway into a new world of expanded perspective, awareness and wisdom.

PUT IT INTO PRACTICE

PRACTICE: Climb to the top of a mountain. Notice how your limited perspective changes as you look out over the valley from a new height.

PRACTICE: Volunteer at a domestic abuse shelter. Watch your problems shrink.

PRACTICE: Learn a new skill or talent that takes years to develop.

PRACTICE: Think of someone who really annoys the heck out of you then imagine them as a small child.

PRACTICE: The next time you feel really bothered with your spouse, child, or co-worker, resist the urge to judge or criticize. Earnestly try to see the situation from their point of view.

PRACTICE: Give a perfect stranger a secret present every week or month. (Anonymously pay for someone's meal at a restaurant or groceries at the market. Leave flowers or fresh bread on someone's front porch.)

PRACTICE: After a difficult day, find a place to be alone. One by one, contemplate God's gifts to you until you relax.

PRACTICE: Spend time groping in the dark, riding in a wheelchair, or wearing ear plugs. Think about the blessing of being able to see, walk or hear.

PRACTICE: Read extensively about other countries and cultures.

PRACTICE: Develop close friendships with people of various ages, nationalities, religions and circumstances.

Inverse Paranoia

"Search diligently, pray always, and be believing, and all things shall work together for your good."

D&C 90:24

$\mathcal{S}ecret \; \#6$

Become an inverse paranoid.

After replacing negative thoughts, calling on God, changing our attitude, feeling more grateful and broadening our perspective, we are now equipped to learn the subtle art of inverse paranoia.

All of us carry a personal story around in our heads. When someone tells you their life story, they unknowingly also tell you if they are a regular, run-of-the-mill paranoid person or a fabulous, one-of-a-kind, inverse paranoid person. A regular run-of-the-mill paranoid person thinks life, experiences and people are out there to get them or do them harm. They are constantly stressed out, negative, anxious and complaining about life—waiting for the other boot to drop. Paranoid people are experts at brooding. They dwell on the past, nurse old wounds, indulge in comparisons, chew on regrets, second guess, obsess on problems and always anticipate the worst-case scenario.

On the other hand, an inverse paranoid person believes life and people are out there to do them good—to a paranoid extent. They are relaxed, positive, believe everyone loves them and that good things are always headed their way. They ask for help when needed, delight in differences, nourish relationships, uplift friends and family, inspire, delight, comfort and charm. When the other boot drops and clobbers them on the noggin, they grab it and go dancing.

For example, if a regular paranoid person tells you their

life story it will go something like this: "My mother was always depressed while I was growing up and my father was obsessed with his career so I grew up shy, insecure and unloved. Then they got divorced and messed me up big time. Then I got married and my husband turned out just like my father and he left me and now all my children are messed up because of their father, and on and on and so forth. You get the picture. This person has written her life story in her mind, and it is a tragedy.

Now, an inverse paranoid person may have the same plot details to work with, but they choose to write their life story more like this: "My mom often glued herself to the bed sheets while I was growing up so I had lots of unstructured time to develop a vivid imagination. I learned great skills in independence and responsibility while I kept the house clean and my siblings fed. 'Who's that?' I asked my mom once when a strange man walked through the living room. 'Why son, that's your father,' my mother answered to my surprise. I knew great things were in store for me because my parents were the perfect character studies for a murder mystery I was going to write when I grew up and became a famous author. After my wife left me, my remarkable children lined me up with a blind date who turned out to be an angel. We got married and I've been living in second heaven every since."

This is basically the same story told through different lenses. When we look through the lens of a camera, we see everything in front of us in the viewfinder. Then we decide what detail to focus on before we take the picture. We can choose to look at our life through a lens that focuses on weaknesses or strengths, blessings or hardships. The picture we take needs to include precisely what we want to emphasize because that picture will become the story of our life. We get to choose whether we want a life story that ends as a tragedy or a masterpiece. A masterpiece doesn't come as the result of all light and no darkness. A masterpiece is darkness that has been dispersed by the light.

When we become an inverse paranoid we assume the person who cuts in front of us on the freeway is hurrying home to a sick child and happily back off. We don't assume bad things about any person or circumstance. We don't realize when someone is trying to annoy or hate us. We assume everyone loves us because we know we're so darn loveable. For example, one woman saw an old acquaintance she hadn't seen for years. She immediately ran up and gave her a hug. That acquaintance bristled and backed off.

"Oh, I forgot you don't like me," the inverse paranoid lady said. "Don't worry. I like you enough for both of us!" Then she gave the woman another hug.

Of course that heartily hugged woman couldn't help herself. She had to laugh. How could she hate someone who liked her so much?

In looking at life through inverse paranoid lenses, we are developing a trust in God that will serve us all our life. How do we start really believing all things will work together for our good? First, we have to desire to believe. Next, we have to do something and ask God to help us. Then finally, we show our trust in God by acting on the promises we are given. After a careful search of the scriptures and our hearts, we commit to face problems as golden opportunities. We move forward with hope and love in the firm belief that God will use all our challenges to our gain. In other words, we believe and act on God's promise to, "search diligently, pray always, and be believing, and all things shall work together for (our) good." (D&C 90:24)

A sense of humor is another important attribute of an inverse paranoid person. Using laughter in difficult situations is like offering ourselves and others the gift of perspective. For example, there was once a famous athlete who received a serious and painful injury while on the playing field. This man had everything wrapped up in his ability to play football. He also possessed everything the world considers important—he was famous, wealthy and had the attention of any woman he wanted. Now it appeared all that was over. I know what I would have been thinking. *Oh, my career! Oh, my money!*

When the team doctors lifted him onto the stretcher, this injured player instead quipped, "You know, my mother was so right. I'm so glad I have on clean underwear!"

We know we're in trouble when we can't see anything humorous or wonderful in our lives. Our belief system should offer us hope and teach us to love, laugh and learn while we're experiencing the inevitable difficulties of life. Being an inverse paranoid means we choose to see the good, no matter what. We relish every day of life. We don't allow any one or any event to take away our love or our joy. We know how precious it is to be granted one more day. We know life is a fragile gift and that time flutters past us like a leaf in the wind, here one minute, then gone on the next breeze. We fully experience the sunshine and the rain and choose to be grateful for both.

PUT IT INTO PRACTICE

PRACTICE: When a car cuts in front of you, back off, smile, wish them well and wave.

PRACTICE: When someone points at you and laughs, immediately assume they must absolutely adore you or admire your engaging personality.

PRACTICE: If you know someone hates you, walk up to them and say, "I think you're wonderful and I know you're just going to love me too when you get to know me better."

PRACTICE: Give yourself or others heartfelt praise and positive affirmations at least daily.

PRACTICE: Disentangle yourself from much-to-do-about-nothing by doing less busy work, shopping less and watching TV less. Then commit to use your time more wisely.

PRACTICE: Every time someone begins talking to you in a negative, critical or complaining way say, "That's interesting. Thank you for sharing. On the other hand, I see it this way." Give that person a more positive, hopeful or loving way to see things.

PRACTICE: Give someone a truly heartfelt hug and be the last one to let go.

PRACTICE: Write your life history. Make it a "masterpiece."

PRACTICE: Always expect something good to happen.

PRACTICE: Relax. Trust God with the ebb and flow of your life.

Muddling Along

"Ye are little children...
and ye cannot bear all
things now; nevertheless,
be of good cheer, for I
will lead you along."

D&C 78:17-18

Secret #7

Give yourself permission to muddle.

After replacing negative thoughts, calling on God, changing our attitude, feeling more gratitude, enlarging our perspective and becoming an inverse paranoid, we can now develop the skills of an expert muddler.

Have you ever had one of those days where you wish you'd stayed in bed? I remember a day like that. The dishwasher had malfunctioned, flooding our house all night as we slept. We didn't know until one of our sleepy-eyed children came into our bedroom early in the morning and said, "Mom and Dad! It's raining in the basement!"

The room that was hardest hit was the storage room where we'd recently carefully stacked and dated our pride and joy, a two-year supply of food. To our horror, everything was quickly being ruined. In a mad dash to save anything we could, every member of the family hauled each bucket and box out into the back yard to dry out. It took hours. Just when we finished, we heard a clap of thunder, looked up and felt several drops splash in our eyes. Then the heavens opened and the few drops immediately became a downpour. We regrouped and quickly hauled our soggy mess into the garage. When we finally got every box and bucket into the garage, my son came running to me in tears, informing me his pet rabbit was dead. After finally getting all the children off to school, my daughter called from campus saying she couldn't remember where she'd parked the car at BYU. Then my other first-grader had an accident that required a change of clothing. To top it off, I fell down a flight of stairs because I was eight months pregnant and very clumsy. You get the picture. Down on my hands and knees wiping up supper that night, I was so exhausted I felt like bursting into tears—but I didn't want to deal with any more water.

"I can't handle it any more," I said to my husband in the other room.

What I really wanted was for my husband to rush to my side, sweep me up in his arms, volunteer to finishing washing the floor, then carry me off to his castle where I'd never have to deal with any problems again.

"You don't have to handle it," my husband said, peering over the newspaper.

"What?!" I replied. "You don't appreciate how hard my life is."

"I mean," Ross answered, "there's no rule book somewhere that says you have to go through life handling everything. Just muddle, Jan. I've been muddling for years and no one can tell the difference."

It is a categorical understatement to say I was flabbergasted at his comment. My husband is a competent bank executive, church leader and a calm and collected father and husband. I couldn't believe my ears. I'd lived with this man every single day for decades and genuinely believed he was always handling everything. Now he confides that he's been muddling? It was difficult to believe. Yet, as I let his words sink inside, it made me feel so much better.

Muddle, I thought. I think I can muddle.

Now every time I'm feeling overwhelmed, I remember Ross's timely advice. Frankly, I've been muddling ever since and so far no one can tell the difference, just like my husband promised. God doesn't want us constantly berating ourselves because of our inadequacies. He doesn't want us to get discouraged with our mistakes or give up when we have a really bad day or a bad decade. He wants us to remember we are His precious children, learning and growing as we go along. God always gives us chances to try again and write a new ending of our story. We're all in this great big

Sunbeam Class trying to be like our heavenly parents. It's not easy, and sometimes we mess up.

I remember a day when I walked into the kitchen to find my young son surrounded by the large white buckets where I stored our flour, rice, sugar and pasta. He was busy scooping—sugar into the flour—rice into the sugar—pasta into the rice—you get the picture. The whole kitchen looked like a white billowing cloud except for my son's innocent grin and two large blue eyes staring up at me.

"Look, Mom. I'm the bread maker!" my young son said as he looked up at me.

Suddenly it dawned on me that whenever I made bread I pulled out all the white buckets and started scooping. He was trying to be like me. My feelings of frustration melted into love. I was so proud of him for trying. As we got busy cleaning the kitchen I realized God loves us like that. No matter how big the mess or mistake we've made, God provides us with a Savior to help us clean it up and make everything all better. We can "be still and know that (He is) God." (Psalm 46:10) That is the essence of muddling. We put our hand into the hand of God's and know in spite of present realities, everything will be all right in the end—no matter what. Christ promises, "Fear not, little children, for you are mine, and I have overcome the world, and you are of them that my Father hath given me; And none of them that my Father hath given me shall be lost." (D&C 50:41-42)

Life often feels like an impossible juggling act. The trick is in knowing how many balls we can keep in the air before it's too many and they all fall down. Most of are too busy with things that don't really matter in the eternal scheme of things. We honestly desire to simplify our lives, but don't know how. We need to give ourselves permission to do less—with more love.

I'm often asked to accompany singing groups on the piano. Because I don't play well, I've been forced to master sight-reading skills. I've found that if I keep the melody going, no one can tell when I miss a few notes here and there with my left hand. It works the same way when we're feeling overwhelmed. If we can identify the melody, we can drop a few commitments and everything works out all right. The melody is love. Without love, nothing else matters or lasts. If we focus on really loving those around us, we won't even notice if they love us back. Even though is seems too good to be true, love really is the only thing that lasts, the only thing worth living and dying for.

Muddling is not mediocrity. Muddling is realizing we all have hard days when we feel fragile and anxious. We all have days when we feel like we're going to break into a million pieces. Muddling is permission to leave control to God. Muddling allows us to stop keeping up appearances or worrying that we'll never measure up. Muddling is accepting our humanness and inadequacies. Muddling is receiving God's love and peace. Muddling is realizing there are some messes only Christ can clean up. Muddling is seeing our worth through God's eyes and never giving up hope that things will work out. We trust God and wait with dignity and courage for the answers. "But they that wait upon the Lord shall renew their strength; they shall mount up with wings as eagles; they shall run, and not be weary; and they shall walk, and not faint." (Isaiah 40:31)

PUT IT INTO PRACTICE

PRACTICE: Create an official certificate granting the recipient permission to muddle. Give it to yourself. Hang it on the wall in a high-traffic place in your home.

PRACTICE: When life gets tough—get soft, real soft.

PRACTICE: Stop doing one activity that gives you stress.

PRACTICE: The next time someone asks you to do something you don't want to do, say no. You simply can't do everything and you can't keep everyone happy.

PRACTICE: Limit multi-tasking. Focus on one thing at a time.

PRACTICE: Develop a fun support network. Get together and play.

PRACTICE: Spend meditative time in nature.

PRACTICE: Relax and say, "This is the reality of my life right now and it is okay."

PRACTICE: Set your own pace. Don't be hurried or pushed by any one.

PRACTICE: If you think you can't do one more thing without falling apart, screaming or crying, you are probably right. So, don't do one more thing.

Funeral Thinking

"Consider the lilies
of the field."

Matthew 6:28

Secret #8

Practice funeral thinking.

After replacing negative thoughts, calling on God, changing our attitude, feeling more gratitude, enlarging our perspective then becoming an inverse paranoid and expert muddler, the next secret to happiness is to seriously contemplate our eventual demise.

I once attended a funeral for a man who lived in my neighborhood. During this man's funeral a short talk was given that changed my life. The man who died taught my class in Sunday School and I enjoyed his lessons immensely. He always taught with an extra dimension of originality, and then topped it off with a sense of humor. His terminal cancer was untimely. He was leaving behind a new wife and young son. Before he died, he asked me if I'd sing at his funeral. Before I could answer, I bawled. He tried to comfort me and told me he was at peace.

"I'll miss snuggling in bed at night with my wife and watching my little boy grow up," he said. "But I trust God. I know everything will turn out all right."

A friend of this man was asked to give a talk at his funeral. While I was sitting near the podium after singing the requested musical number, this friend walked haltingly to the microphone. He shook with emotion as he stood awkwardly at the pulpit preparing to begin. Whenever he tried to speak a flood of emotion would overwhelm him. He'd pull himself together before he'd try again. This happened over and over for a good five minutes. Five minutes behind a pulpit without saying anything tends to get the audience's attention. We were all praying for him. Finally this man was able to utter three words. Those three words changed my life.

"He loved me," this friend said with tears streaming down his face.

That was all he was able to utter before he sat down. Those three words were the sole text of the most beautiful sermon I've ever heard. It occurred to me that if someone could say those three words about me when I died, I will have lived a meaningful life. I'd previously thought my value depended on how many people loved me, not how many people I loved. Because of that talk I realized that love loses its power when we expect something back. We love best when we let go expectations of what we want in return. Since that day at the funeral, I made a decision to live the rest of my life as a student studying the miracle of love.

The only people who are truly happy are those who have learned to live for others. When we truly love others, we are perceptive about their relationship to their own lives and not overly concerned about their relationship to our lives. We love them because they exist, not because they earn it. Only God offers us unconditional love—the rest of us are just practicing. When we are filled with God's love, we always have enough to share. What will really matter when we die—the kind of house we lived in, car we drove or how much money we had in the bank? No. Our lives will have meaning only if we've taken the time to truly love someone.

My husband and I like to go for walks around the cemetery. Looking at the markers is always good for personal perspective adjustments. I often stop and read the headstones. The limited space on the grave marker demands the surviving loved ones limit their descriptions of the departed to a few words like "loving mother" – "gentle husband" – "precious child." What few words do we want to describe us? When I read the simple phases chiseled in the granite, I always leave with a clearer focus about what matters most. Our ability to love those closest to us will determine the quality of our life.

Who will hold us in their arms when we die? Who will care

that we lived at all? Who will miss our presence? Why do we so often spend time on things that matter least instead of people who matter most? When we focus our time, energy and affection on people, we have the same priorities as our Creator.

My husband and I attended a graveside service for a tiny baby born to our friends. I remember standing silently at the freshly dug grave with other family members and friends when the limousine drove up. When the funeral-home operator opened the long car door, we saw our friends inside. The new father was gently cradling the tiny coffin on his lap. The new mother, only a few days from a hard delivery and birth, sat motionless—her face white and still, her eyes red and tired. This was their first child, a son. Our friends were two gentle, quiet, sensitive people we'd known in high school. They'd waited a long time for this baby. It was a simple graveside service. The wind was icy cold as our friends slipped their arms around each other so tightly their knuckles went white. Together, they quietly and graciously acknowledged each condolence, reserving their grief for solitude.

I left that service with an urgency to thank God for the gift of my children. Funerals and cemeteries remind us that life is fragile. The secret is to savor each moment. We are given this day and only this day. The past is gone and the future in uncertain. The present moment is a holy gift. When we reach of the end of our life, will we be at peace with ourselves and with God? Becoming a loving person is the only lasting legacy.

The older I get and the more funerals I attend, the more I realize how few people really care when someone dies. Without a close family and friends, one passing life doesn't seem to create that much interest. I am slowly learning what it means to live and love so that those around me will become heart of my heart and soul of my soul. What I desire most in this life is that those around me know I love them. Life has taught me that love only fails me when I don't give it. Sharing my love—whether or not it is returned—always fills me with peace and joy. All real joy is in the moment. All true peace is in us. We don't have to die to have heaven on earth—only love.

PUT IT INTO PRACTICE

PRACTICE: When you attend your next funeral, really listen to what is said about the departed. Determine to change your focus to what matters most in life.

PRACTICE: Go to a cemetery and read the headstones.

PRACTICE: Contemplate the meaning of life and death.

PRACTICE: Ask yourself, "If I died tomorrow, what would I leave undone?" Then, do it today or make plans to see it happen soon.

PRACTICE: Write your own life history and obituary then live the rest of your life to fulfill what you said about yourself.

PRACTICE: Decide today, what you want to do with the rest of your life.

PRACTICE: Act as though this day is your last day of earth—it may be.

PRACTICE: Slow down and savor the moment, today!

PRACTICE: Begin and end each day with thanksgiving and prayer.

PRACTICE: Decide what words you want on your headstone.

Adjustment Patterns

"Wherefore, be of good
cheer, and do not fear, for
I the Lord am with you,
and will stand by you."

D&C 68:6

Secret #9

Develop healthy adjustment patterns.

After replacing negative thoughts, calling on God, changing our attitude, feeling gratitude, enlarging our perspective, becoming an inverse paranoid, muddling and funeral thinking we can take a close look at our personal adjustment patterns. An adjustment pattern is the way we habitually respond to stress.

Most of us developed adjustment patterns in childhood. Some of these coping skills are healthy and some are unhealthy. For example, perhaps you woke up one morning and suddenly remembered you had in test in school that day and you hadn't studied. Your stomach turned over and you felt a lot of anxiety as you contemplated the outcome of your procrastination. So you told your mother you didn't feel well and didn't want to go to school that day. Your mother looked at you and believed you. Your problem was solved. You learned you could get out of difficult situations by being sick. So the next time something stressful comes along, you get sick. This pattern continues into adulthood, and before long you're not even aware you're doing it.

There is hope. Unhealthy patterns of adjustment can be acknowledged and changed into healthy coping skills. One woman told me she used to make her husband listen to long lists of his character flaws. Her husband responded by defending himself. She had learned to deal with troubling emotions and relationship issues when she was a child by watching her parents berate each other. She knew no other way. Now as an adult, she felt chronically frustrated with her husband because he never listened attentively or attempted any significant change.

One day just after she finished another verbal beating, her husband responded by saying, "Honey, did it occur to you that I could come up with a list of your faults, too?"

This woman told me she was dumbfounded because she had never considered her husband's point of view. The next time she felt like reading her husband a long list of his faults, she tried seeing matters from his perspective. She consciously took a good look at herself and what she was doing that contributed to the friction in their relationship. When she did this, her mind was filled with positive actions she could take to improve their relationship. This woman has successfully changed a negative pattern of adjustment into a positive coping skill that serves her well.

There was a man who was in love and was about to get married, when his fiancé suddenly dumped him and married his best friend. He was devastated. He grew more and more depressed, gradually retreated into seclusion and eventually killed himself. This is unhealthy adjustment. There was another man in the same situation who was also deeply in love with his fiancé and about to get married when she dumped him and married his best friend. He was also devastated. He felt depressed, but decided he'd feel better if he focused on someone else. He volunteered at the hospital where he met a wonderful, caring woman. A year later, they got married. This is healthy adjustment.

Suicide is an extreme example of an unhealthy adjustment pattern, but it serves to illustrate this fact—bad things happen to all of us. We don't always get to choose what happens to us, but we always choose how we respond. We can focus on ourselves and what we've lost or we can focus on others and what remains. Maybe we haven't considered taking our own life but do we habitually take offense, get angry, seek revenge, become bitter or judgmental, or allow our fears to control us? All these responses to problems are a pattern of adjustment we formed years ago. Now is the time to change our unhealthy patterns into healthy ones.

68

When we are living through a major period of stress it helps to pay attention to how we treat ourselves. Self-nurturance is a healthy adjustment pattern. We are more likely to respond positively to challenges if we are taking good care of ourselves. We need to develop our own private way to unwind, such as spending time in nature, praying or reading to a child. We need not constantly rush to fill the inexhaustible demands of work, family or church and community duties.

God will give us the ability to adjust positively to any situation—if we ask for help. God can help us laugh when we feel like crying. We simply can't control events or people, only ourselves. At times of change, loss or adjustment, we don't have to rely on our own strength. "He giveth power to the faint; and to them that have no might he increaseth strength." (Isaiah 40:29)

One of my friends told me she had battled depression her whole life. She'd tried counseling and medication but nothing seemed to help. Then she discovered when she played the piano her depression lifted. She now plays beautiful music at rest homes.

I had another friend who was constantly upset with her husband because he wouldn't talk to her. She was certain that if her husband really loved her, he would have long, heartfelt conversations with her. Well, her husband was a quiet man. For thirty years she was frustrated. One evening it came to a breaking point. She told him she'd had enough. If he didn't talk to her, she was going to leave him. What did her husband do? He promptly stood up and walked out of the room. Her threats got louder as she chased him to the front door. Finally in desperation she lunged forward and hit him on the back of the head. I learned about this experience when I saw her sitting in church with her hand in a cast.

"What happened?" I asked.

"Want the truth or what I've been telling everybody else?" she answered.

"The truth."

"I hit my husband and broke two fingers."

She was obviously embarrassed. She turned to me and tearfully said, "I've been trying to get him to talk to me for thirty years. I just couldn't stand it any more. I couldn't bear to watch him walk out on me one more time."

Now, I am also married to a quiet man, so I said, "Want some ideas?" She sheepishly nodded. "The next time you feel you have to talk to your husband so desperately you're going to burst, go for a walk instead," I said. "Then talk to God. Ask God if He loves you. Be still and listen until you feel God's love. No one else can give you that kind of unconditional love. The rest of us are just practicing." She stared at me, puzzled. "Then after you feel divine love, ask God how to love your husband."

I promised her she would be filled with positive impressions of her husband's strengths instead of his weaknesses. I promised her that when she finished walking, she'd feel more love for herself and her husband. I didn't see this woman for a few months. When I saw her at church, her cast was off and she was holding hands with her husband while she walked down the hall. She winked at me.

"Thank you!" she said enthusiastically. "And I've lost ten pounds!"

Whether we pray, go for a walk or play beautiful music at rest homes, positive patterns of adjustment can and will give us more joy in our mortal journey. Carefully chosen coping techniques give us tools to live with power, dignity and energy. We're all gong to meet with frustrations and pain. The important thing is what we do when faced with problems like financial failure, scandal, divorce, abuse, death, way-ward children, chronic ill-health issues, old age and any other of a million problems or challenges. Everyone does something. Some people turn into hermits. Others turn to drugs, sickness or chronic victim-hood. We can choose to turn to God, learn about the nature of love and press forward. The scriptures refer to this as enduring to the end—to which I add, enduring well to the end.

The American Red Cross trains their volunteers to help people involved in trauma to focus on how they survived instead of going over the trauma that occurred. That way they are reinforcing coping skills rather than reliving the horror of the experience. Whether our traumas are large or small, we can refuse to get discouraged by our efforts to survive and overcome. Even when our efforts are not showing fruits in the present, the desires of our hearts are known to God and sacred. There is dignity in the struggles of life if we face them with optimism and hope. We can renew our emotional and physical weariness with strength when we rely on our Creator.

No one is always well-adjusted. I used to wear a sweatshirt around with a mallard duck print on the front. The duck's head was on backward. Underneath the duck was this word, mallard-justed. Sometimes we all feel like our heads are on backward or we're being slowly pecked to death. That's when we need to turn to God and renew our strength. We are all maladjusted to a certain degree and in a perpetual state of fine-tuning. Problems will keep happening as long as we are still alive. It helps to remember we win some and we lose some. There is no easy time of life.

Each of us can choose our own coping skills or adjustment patterns when we feel overwhelmed, anxious, stressed out or downhearted. We may choose to go for a long sweaty run, lie in a hammock, play a round of golf, sing opera in the shower or write a long narrative in our journal. There is a battle for our souls and that battle plays out in our minds. We have to face the enemy and kill those negative, wounded and fearful thoughts like a courageous soldier. The audacity of hope and optimism is the only way to develop positive adjustment patterns that will change our lives—and eventually change the world.

PUT IT INTO PRACTICE

PRACTICE: Uncover an unhealthy adjustment pattern you have developed. Change it into one that is positive.

PRACTICE: Treat yourself to something new and uplifting that you've never experienced before in food, entertainment, reading material, sports or recreation.

PRACTICE: Constantly stay in the learning mode all your life through reading, teaching or taking lessons and classes.

PRACTICE: The next time you're in over your head, ask for help.

PRACTICE: When life gets too tough, go for a walk, take a bubble bath, see a funny movie or read a humorous book.

PRACTICE: When you feel most like getting even, don't.

PRACTICE: Discover for yourself if your current addiction is really a cover to keep you from feeling hurt. We have to feel the pain before we can feel the joy.

PRACTICE: Don't do the same things over and over and expect a different result. That is the definition of crazy.

PRACTICE: Decide if you are living in a rut. If so, regularly try something new, scary or uncomfortable.

PRACTICE: Write all your worry thoughts on paper—groan, then burn them.

Smiling Adventures

"A merry heart maketh a
cheerful countenance."

Proverbs 15:13

Secret #10

Smile.

After replacing negative thoughts, calling on God, changing our attitude, feeling more gratitude, enlarging our perspective, becoming an inverse paranoid, muddling, contemplating death, and developing healthy adjustment patterns, we are free to offer others our own personal sunshine by smiling.

On the other hand, getting other people to smile on demand is a bit tricky. Attempts to get my sizeable family bathed, dressed and looking pleasant for a picture is like medieval torture. Just saying the words "family portrait" makes me break out in a cold sweat. When my non-enthusiastic family is finally lined up for this mother-initiated activity, I feel great compassion for our frazzled photographer.

"Pull that finger out of your nose," the photographer says. "Would the teenager on the back row take off the sun glasses? Now everybody, look at me. You in the black suit—quit giving your wife finger antlers. Now on the count of three, everybody look at me and say pickles. One, two, three—pickles!"

Pickles? Why pickles? Because saying that word makes people smile. Try it. Why do we want to see ourselves smiling in pictures? Why not just snap a realistic photo of family members milling around showing their true mood at the moment? Because we all look and feel better when we smile. So why don't we do it more often?

While insisting others smile can be a cause of great frustration, getting ourselves to smile will always bring us joy. If you want to conduct a truly magical experiment try this. Look each person you encounter in the eye and then smile. Do this even if you don't feel like it and whether or not your life is running smoothly at the moment. Do this with family members and total strangers. Notice how smiling makes you feel.

When we smile, we send the signal to our brain that we're happy. Our body responds to what we think and pretty soon we are happy. We feel more relaxed and radiant when we smile. Also observe the responses you receive after you smile. Most people will smile back. Will you receive a few odd looks? Yes, but don't let that discourage you. Why do most people smile back? Because when someone smiles, we assume they're thinking a kind thought about us. Smiling is contagious. The more smiles we give away, the more smiles we receive in return.

I remember a time when I was worried about one of my teenage sons. I prayed long and hard asking God to teach me how to love my son. The impression I received was simple—smile. This answer perplexed me. Still, I gave it a try. I began smiling at my son more often. I made an effort to catch his eye and smile at him during breakfast and at supper. Before he left for school, I hugged, kissed and smiled at him. When he was driving away in the car, I waved and smiled. When he got home, I smiled. Something happened to me because of those smiles. I felt more love for my son. My heart softened toward him. I noticed myself appreciating him more and becoming keenly aware of his courage in the face of adolescence. I wasn't sure at the time if he noticed or if it meant anything to him. Teenage boys aren't famous for expressing tender emotions. Some time later I received a letter from this son who had become an adult.

"Dear Mom, thank you for smiling at me. When I was making my most difficult decisions I would see your face in my mind, smiling," he wrote. "I knew you loved me and it made all the difference."

Smiling creates an instant connection—a universal language

that says, "Hi! I notice you. I like what I see." Smiling is something positive we do that elevates our thoughts and the thoughts of the one receiving the smile. Grinning helps the person we smile at feel noticed, accepted and validated. Yes, some chronically grouchy people will be suspicious and will not respond in kind—but even then we can drive them crazy wondering what we're up to.

Like learning to play a musical instrument, smiling will not come naturally at first. If we want to get good at something, we have to practice. When I played the violin for the first time, I didn't know how to hold the bow or where to place my fingers on the strings. The sound I produced was scratchy and ear piercing. Likewise, our first cautious smiles won't instantly produce a sudden change in life as we know it. In fact we may feel uncomfortable and even embarrassed at first. Most people start out smiling tentatively— ready to take back their smile if it's not returned. If we keep trying, our efforts to smile easily and often will soon become a habit. The more we smile, the more others will be drawn to us. Smiling and receiving a smile is a simple moment of connected joy.

Smiling is also the forerunner of laughter. In fact, our ability to laugh is serious business. Did you know scientists have discovered if we suppress our laughter, it sucks back down into our body and spreads out at our hips? When we radiate happiness, it is reflected back to us. The opposite is also true. Remember the last time you felt grouchy? Wasn't it amazing how everybody around you seemed to be having a bad day as well? In the morning when my children leave for school instead of saying, "Have a great day," I say, "Make it a great day. The choice is yours!"

When is the last time you laughed so hard your face hurt, your eyes watered and your nose ran? When is the last time you did something really dumb or embarrassing then laughed yourself silly right away instead of waiting for ten years to see the humor in the situation? When is the last time you shared a funny story or joke instead of your latest tragedy or ailment?

Smiling is also a great way to meet new people. I've learned strangers are just future friends I haven't smiled at yet. Once I was sitting in the Marriott Center at BYU during a Women's

Conference. I was one of the speakers that day but none of my family or friends could make it to listen to my talk. I was feeling sad and alone even though there were thousands of women all around me. At that very moment, the woman sitting next to me turned and smiled. I smiled back.

"You have such beautiful skin," she said.

Shocked, I looked into her kind eyes and answered, "Thank you."

It felt like she'd tossed me a ball of sunshine. My usual response would be to dismiss a compliment with something like, "My skin? Are you kidding? I have such greasy skin and I still get zits." Yet that day I felt the need to accept her gift with the same graciousness it was offered. I could tell she was sincere. In the end, it didn't really matter what she said. She could have said, "You have such beautiful hangnails." What mattered was that she smiled at me, acknowledged I existed and said something kind to me. Instantly, I no longer felt alone or sad any more. I had the impression that if this woman and I knew each other, we would be friends. It occurred to me that I was surrounded by family and friends. I just hadn't met or smiled at them yet.

We unlock our personal power for good when we offer the gift of a genuine and loving smile. Turning up the corners of our mouths helps us spread sunshine every where we go. So on those days when we feel less than, worried, diminished, sad or lonely—we need to get out there and start smiling. I've learned my day usually goes the same way as the corners of my mouth.

PUT IT INTO PRACTICE

PRACTICE: Make a decision to smile at everyone you encounter for a day. Notice how people react and how you feel.

PRACTICE: Pull weird faces at the person staring back at you in the mirror.

PRACTICE: Get your picture taken posing with a silly expression.

PRACTICE: Wear your pajamas to the grocery store, give out candy and a smile to everyone you see.

PRACTICE: Read the comics before you read the front page.

PRACTICE: Collect media and entertainment that makes you smile.

PRACTICE: Make up a silly song and sing it in front of an audience.

PRACTICE: Forget yourself and develop a genuine interest in the other people. Your smile becomes warmer and more spontaneous.

PRACTICE: Send a funny card to someone who needs a lift.

PRACTICE: The next time you feel sad, force yourself to smile. Then go do something nice for somebody.

Grin and Share

"In the world ye shall
have tribulation: but be
of good cheer; I have
overcome the world."

_____

John 16:33

$\mathcal{S}ecret\ \#11$

Go from grin and bear it to grin and share it.

After replacing negative thoughts, calling on God, changing our attitude, feeling more grateful, deepening our perspective, becoming an inverse paranoid, muddling, funeral thinking, developing healthy adjustment patterns and smiling, we can discover what great fun it is to share our goof-ups and mistakes.

One of the most amazing mathematical facts your algebra teacher never taught you is this: catastrophe + time = humor. The quicker we laugh about and share the embarrassing or humiliating events in our lives, the sooner we'll relax and enjoy life. When we stop worrying about our public image, we begin living authentically. We don't have to grit our teeth and endure life white-knuckled, afraid of looking incompetent or foolish to our friends, associates and family. Why? Because people actually relate to us better when we're a dufus. All of us have felt inept at times. Nobody feels perfectly put-together and competent; we all have a slight inferiority complex. When we try to appear flawless, we give a false impression that intimidates others.

For example, once my family was asked to sing a musical number in church. I didn't want to look incompetent so I made my large, unruly brood practice for several months until I was sure we were ready to perform flawlessly. Needless to say, events did not go as planned. When it came time for us to perform, I lined my little ones in front of the microphone on a stool and placed the older children behind them. My husband stood at the side holding the baby so he could make sure no one bolted for the door.

I sat down on the piano and was almost ready to begin my introduction when my young son on the front row suddenly sucked the entire microphone into his mouth and yelled, "Ahhh-OOOO-GA!!!"

I watched in horror as my husband set the baby down so he could de-suction our toddler from the microphone. Then the baby ran over to the piano and started banging on the keys. At this point the other little kids on the front row got the giggles so bad that snot foamed out their nostrils. The older children on the back row were so humiliated they were a member of our embarrassing family that they turned a deep shade of red, vowing to change their last name and move into an orphanage.

To this day, I can't remember if we actually sang the song we'd meticulously prepared for that day. I was so embarrassed I don't recall what actually happened after that. What I do remember is that I've never received so many compliments. I learned other people don't expect our public performances to be perfect and, in fact, they are more entertaining when something goes wrong.

"That was the best musical number we've had in this ward for years," was the sentiment I heard expressed from dozens of giggling ward members. The whole congregation seemed energized, happier and friendlier to each other that day. It dawned on me that my fellow church goers had not judged me as an incompetent mother saddled with uncontrollable, obnoxious children—they actually enjoyed the whole bumbling Baadsgaard performance. If we're going to look goofy anyway, why waste so much time trying to appear like we're not?

These days I actually enjoy showing up to any family performance to see what embarrassing or goofy things we are going to do this time. The day I quit trying to orchestrate or control what was going to happen was the day I began enjoying my life. Think about it—what do we talk about around the dinner table or when we visit with friends? We generally share the most embarrassing events in our lives. So why don't we just laugh about them when they happen? If we had performed flawlessly that Sunday, our family musical number would have been quickly forgotten. Instead we are now recorded in the annals of church history. Everybody loved us for just trying. Why? Because we've all been there. We've all forgotten to zip up our pants, been turned down for a date, or failed a test. It makes us feel better when we see we're not alone.

Our family slogan is: "If you keep both feet on the ground, you can't get your pants on!" I like that slogan because it reminds me to take life lightly. To move from "grin and bear it" to "grin and share it" we need to surround ourselves with positive people and choose life-affirming activities. I'm usually way too serious, so I purposely write humorous family life newspaper columns, magazine articles and books to help me live on the bright side. If we're naturally dour we need to practice laughing especially at ourselves by telling jokes, embarrassing stories or making up funny slogans. Laugher is a great form of exercise—like jogging on the inside.

We can get more mileage from our muff-ups and mistakes by sharing them. For example, the day I backed into my husband's company truck with our family van in our own driveway was not a stellar moment. I instantly knew we'd have to pay for both repairs out-of-pocket. I felt so deeply dumb it leaked out my eyeballs. A man in my neighborhood dropped off his little girl to play with my daughter about an hour later. Dumbness was still leaking from my eyes when he arrived.

"What's wrong?" he asked. When I told him, he laughed. His reaction was not what I expected. "Hey that's nothing," he continued. "You should have seen the look on this guy's face when I pulled him over and forgot to put my patrol car in park. I was standing there writing him a speeding ticket when suddenly—bam! The poor guy got a speeding ticket and his new car rear-ended by the deputy sheriff in less than a minute. Not exactly a shining moment for the department."

After hearing his story, I laughed out loud. Suddenly my driveway crash didn't seem so bad any more. I instantly liked this deputy a lot more after he told me his story. Why? He became human to me. He was he no longer an intimidating, straight-faced officer with a gun just waiting behind the corner to catch me doing something stupid. He did dumb things just like me.

"Hey," I answered, "once I managed to wreck our car all by myself without even leaving our garage! It cost thousands to fix it!"

We went on trying to top each other with all the dumb things we'd done with our motor vehicles until we were both in stitches. The point here is that we both felt a lot better that day after we shared all our not-so-brilliant goof-ups. Why? Humor builds bridges, relieves stress and promotes health. The next time you do something really dumb don't try to hide it. Blab it to everyone you see that day. Chances are you'll learn all the goofy things everybody else has done and you'll both feel a whole lot better.

Researchers have discovered that laughter can actually lower blood pressure and trigger a flood of endorphins. Endorphins are brain chemicals that bring on a feeling of well-being and even euphoria. Laughter also affects our immune system. Gamma-interferon, a disease-fighting protein, rises with laughter. So do B-cells, which produce disease-destroying antibodies and T-cells, which orchestrate our body's immune response. Laughter can also shut off the flow of stress hormones that come into play when we feel hostility, rage or stress. Stress hormones suppress the immune system, raise blood pressure, and increase the number of platelets in the blood which can cause fatal artery blockage. Keeping a sense of humor really is serious business.

There are literally hundreds of ways to invite joy and laughter into your life without waiting until everything is going smoothly, because it never will. Finding humor can be learned, practiced, reinforced and internalized just like any other skill. Everyone has an innate sense of humor, although it may be hidden after years of neglect. Remember, those who laugh—last. Humor is an effective way to manage stress and prevent burnout. Stress is caused by our perception of events not the actual events. We can't control what happens to us but we can control our perception of what happens to us through humor. That is power through perspective.

If we can find humor in something, we can survive it. People who are dour and gloomy exacerbate their illnesses and shorten their life spans. Laugher is as good as exercise. To stay healthy we not only have to eat right, we have to think right. Happy people treat stress as a positive challenge rather than a negative event. Being able to laugh at ourselves is mentally healthy.

By developing a sense of humor, we can increase our ability to tap creative problem-solving abilities. Humor can be an affectionate communication of insight. Using humor is one way to lobby for change without being offensive. One wife found if she clutched her heart and threw herself on the floor yelling, "Oh, you're so right, it's killing me!" when she and her husband started arguing, the steam suddenly left the conflict. Another woman took out a classified ad that read, "Husband for sale, cheap. Comes complete with hunting and fishing equipment, one pair of jeans, two shirts, black Lab retriever and too many pounds of venison. Pretty good guy, but not home much from October to December and from April to October. Will consider trade." After approximately 66 telephone calls, some of them serious, the wife placed another ad: "Retraction of husband for sale cheap. Everybody wants the dog, not the husband."

Humor is also an effective way to communicate serious messages with a light touch. For example, there was a woman who was always losing her glasses. So she decided to use humor to solve her problem. She pasted a note to her glasses case that read, "If you have these, I don't. They are owned by a little old lady who is driving home among your loved ones. Please return." Then she included her name and address. After she put that note on her glasses, the person who found them always quickly returned them.

Love may make the world go around, but laughter keeps us from getting so dizzy we want to get off. Humor is everywhere if we're paying attention. Take for example the notice in the church bulletin board that read, "There will be meetings in the north and south ends of the church. Children will be baptized on both ends." Or the sign on a hospital bulletin board that observed, "Research shows that the first five minutes of life can be the most risky." Penciled underneath, "The last five minutes are pretty risky too." Or the cartoon of a doctor consulting with a patient that read, "I think the problem is your gall bladder, but if you want on a second opinion, Ill say it's your kidneys."

There are circumstances in life we can change and circumstances we can't. Humor helps us effectively deal with both. We don't have to grin and bear it, we can grin and share it. We'll discover life is so much more fun when we share more than we bear. Humor can be a wonderful way to add years to our life and life to our years—by preventing a hardening of the attitudes. Laugher is the jest medicine.

PUT IT INTO PRACTICE

PRACTICE: Share an embarrassing story with family, friends and co-workers.

PRACTICE: The next time you feel like complaining about your latest health problem, don't do it until you can tell it in a story that will make people laugh.

PRACTICE: When you do something stupid, blab is to everybody. You'll feel a lot better and so will they.

PRACTICE: Try using humor in your most trying relationship. If nothing changes, at least you'll be having more fun.

PRACTICE: Tell your friends what body part you are most self-conscious about.

PRACTICE: Tell your children about the time when you had a crush on somebody, failed a test or got in trouble for doing something wrong.

PRACTICE: View your kitchen table with more reverence and importance. Share relaxed and spirited meal time conversations. Start traditions, play games, celebrate holidays, offer prayers, nourish souls and invoke all the richest blessings of feasting into your home. If you live alone invite company on a regular basis.

PRACTICE: When you are eating at a fancy dinner party, entertain the guests by turning your eyelids or lips inside out.

PRACTICE: Create a stand-up comedy routine that forces you to laugh about the difficulties in life you are experiencing.

PRACTICE: Write a light-hearted family Christmas newsletter where you share your goof-ups instead of your achievements.

Can Do

"I can do all things
through Christ which
strengtheneth me."

Philippians 4:13

Secret # 12

Do things you think you can't do.

After replacing negative thoughts, calling on God, changing our attitude, feeling more grateful, deepening our perspective, becoming an inverse paranoid, muddling, funeral thinking, developing healthy adjustment patterns, smiling and sharing mistakes we can now muster the courage to do things we think we can't do.

While I was growing up, I always wanted to play in the school orchestra. I begged my mother, but she told me only rich kids played expensive instruments. So I sang in the choir instead. Singing didn't cost anything. Well, I grew up, got married, and it took me thirty years to get all my children in school. I thought I'd missed my chance. Then at 52 I quit using old excuses and joined the New Horizons Orchestra. This is a unique orchestra. They welcome beginners.

When I began playing the violin, the music I produced resembled sick birds with scratchy sore throats—but I kept trying. As I practiced I felt areas of my brain wake up and form new connections. My fingers drummed note placements on my bed pillow at night. I heard the melody I was learning drifting through my mind at odd times, like when I was driving the car or doing the dishes. As the orchestra director gently guided us through our first elementary songs, there were moments when the music seemed to lift from the page and wrap around my heart. During the pauses, the moments of quiet between the notes, I felt aroused and elevated—

like flying without leaving the ground. The learning process was not intimidating or humiliating; it was energizing, exhilarating and fun. After we played our first song in three parts, I jumped from my seat exclaiming, "We're an orchestra! We make music!"

One woman had a brain tumor, resulting in the removal of large portions of her brain. She went into a deep depression that didn't lift until her husband brought her to our orchestra. As she learned to play an instrument, her brain developed new pathways and many other abilities came back to her. An eighty-six year old woman crippled with arthritis also became a member of the orchestra. Though her fingers were gnarled, she persisted and learned to play the violin before she died.

We're never too old, young, dumb or poor to learn something new. Studies show people rarely try anything new after the age of forty. Good grief, we have to be that old before we're wise enough to let go of all the status symbols in our culture and start living an authentic life. It's never time to have a midlife crisis. It's always time to have an all-life awakening. An all-life awakening invites us to learn something new at every age.

When we have a new experience physically it will take us to new territory mentally. When we let go of routine and venture into the discomfort of being a beginner, it opens dormant mental power. We feel more enthusiasm, energy and excitement for other areas of our life as well. The power of learning and experiencing new things is contagious. Learning in one area always ignites learning in another. If we are always learning or experiencing something new it keeps us in touch with how it feels during the change process. When we were children, each day presented us with something challenging. We were constantly required to change, adapt and grow. Then we became adults, eased into a comfortable rut and got stuck in stability, stagnation and safety. The wonder, curiosity and sparkle left our eyes.

All of us know someone who is old in years but still retains their zest for living. They're fun to be around. How do they do it? They have the courage to keep trying new things. How do we get this childhood liveliness back? Learn or experience something new.

It takes humility and courage to be a beginner at any age. "Oh, I could never do that," I hear people say when I invite them to try something. I always tell them they will never know if they never try. I hear lots of excuses—money, time, ability, talents, illness and age. In fact, if we really want to do something, we'll find a way.

Others often invite us to learn something new by asking us to do things beyond our capability. Responding positively to invitations to serve others always leads to personal growth. For example, when I was a teenager, I was often asked to play the piano at church. I desperately needed time to practice before I could play any piece well. Most of the choristers gave me the music ahead of time. One chorister never did. Needless to say, I was stressed out because I didn't want to look like an idiot in front of my peers. One day I was asked to play a hymn roughly six seconds before crunch time. I turned to the hymn and discovered it had four sharps. I immediately panicked and quickly prayed, "Heavenly Father, help! I can't do four sharps!"

What followed was the quickest personal revelation I've ever received. "Just pretend it's in three flats and I'll help you." Naïve and desperate I followed that impression without question. I played the hymn written in four sharps in three flats and it sounded all right! Well, that was sufficient proof of another Red Sea parting for me. It wasn't until 35 years later that someone told me you can change the flats into sharps and the sharps into flats as long as they add up to seven.

Actually, I failed to appreciate the real miracle—God knew me. God knew me well enough to know I thought I could play that song in three flats. I was given a way to think about my challenge in a way I could survive it. The Creator of this universe who has to keep the cosmos going knows all of us that intimately. How much good could we do with our lives if we accept invitations to serve others, then let go of our fears and depend on God for our strength? God will give us a way to think about our challenges in a way that we can handle it—if we ask.

Our heavenly parents know and love us better than we know and love ourselves. We are never asked to bear any challenge alone.

There are many things we're absolutely sure we can't face, such as the death of a love one, chronic illness, financial failure, spouse betrayal or wayward children. Yet life often requires us to face what we fear most. When we live through the very trial we hoped to avoid, we have the opportunity to learn, grow and receive God's infinite love for us. When we feel the love of God, there is nothing left to fear.

Sometimes when we are faced with difficult times, we just need extra gripping power. Tiny green plums in my back yard taught me this lesson. One spring, I was experiencing a difficult time emotionally and physically after the death of a loved one. One morning I walked out into our back yard and noticed hundreds of miniature green plums just beginning to form on our fruit tree. That tiny, undeveloped fruit represented the harvest we hoped to reap later in the summer. My mouth watered just thinking about their tart and sweet taste.

That night there was a huge storm. I heard the wind howling, twisting and wailing all night long while I lay in bed unable to sleep. The next day when I walked outside, I noticed piles of green plums blown from the tree in the storm disappearing into the grass. They let go. I looked closely to see what remained. There were still a few tiny plums clinging tightly to the tree branches. All that spring I watched and waited. Those few tiny plums grew and ripened. The fruit that survived and drew strength from the tree throughout the growing season had one important quality—they hung on. That ability alone made the difference. Now when I'm experiencing an unexpected loss, I always pray for strength to hold on. I draw on strength beyond myself and beyond this world. I know in time my harvest will come.

If we practice doing things we think we can't do, we will discover that with time and divine help—we can. Whether we have to face the loss of a loved one, learn a new musical instrument or simply hang on through trying circumstances, we can accomplish and bear so much more than we suppose. We never have to give up hope. Everything that happens in our lives can be used as a lesson if we are ready to be taught.

PUT IT INTO PRACTICE

PRACTICE: Learn to play a musical instrument.

PRACTICE: Do something new that scares the heck out of you.

PRACTICE: Master a new language.

PRACTICE: Run in a marathon, get out of debt, clean the garage or something else you think is impossible.

PRACTICE: Climb a mountain.

PRACTICE: Go back to school.

PRACTICE: Cook something new every night for a week.

PRACTICE: Sing a solo in front of strangers.

PRACTICE: Take a trip to the place in the world you've always wanted to go.

PRACTICE: Be aware that you already possess all the wisdom, power, strength and creativity to make your dreams come true.

Becoming Childlike

"Except ye be converted, and
become as little children,
ye shall not enter into the
kingdom of heaven."

Matthew 18:3

Secret # 13

Become more childlike.

After replacing negative thoughts, calling on God, changing our attitude, feeling gratitude, deepening our perspective, becoming an inverse paranoid, muddling, funeral thinking, developing healthy adjustment patterns, smiling, sharing mistakes and doing new things we graduate to learning how to become like a child again.

One day my little girl had just finished her bath. I turned my head just in time to see her leaping gracefully down the hall in sheer ecstasy—buck naked.

"Oh, Momma! I feel just like one of those wild horses," she said, smiling.

I stopped and wondered, "When was the last time I leaped down the hall buck naked and felt like one of those wild horses? When was the last time I looked in the mirror and even smiled?" When Christ told us we needed to become as a child to enter the kingdom of heaven, He was teaching us what qualities of character are important. Children have a fresh perspective that always delights.

One day my young son left for school wearing bright, rainbow-colored moon boots that were in style roughly two decades earlier—hand-me-downs from older siblings. When he got home he told me the boys at school had called him "stupid boots."

"I'm sorry you had a bad day," I answered.

"Oh, I didn't have a bad day," he said. "Just a bad ten seconds.

The rest of the day was pretty great. I don't care what those guys say. These boots are awesome."

Children are naturally resilient and can be such great role models. Once while I knelt with my three-year-old as she said her prayers, she suddenly and without my prompting told her Heavenly Father a knock-knock joke. After her amen, I must have look a little stunned because she tried to reassure me.

"Don't worry Mom. Heavenly Father likes to laugh sometimes, you know."

Research shows adults laugh only a few times a day. Children laugh hundreds of times a day! When you look at that statistic it makes adulthood seem repressed and inhibited. Let's appreciate children as the magnificent teachers they really are.

One of my children used to pray every day at the dinner table, "Dear Heavenly Father, please help us all be more huggable today."

You know, I really tried to be more huggable after I said amen to her prayers. Children offer their affection without scrutiny. They live in the present and are curious, observant and look freshly at common things. Children are our greatest teachers of love. My children have taught me the simple essence of a meaningful life.

Adults have grown accustomed to ignoring each other. When we walk down a sidewalk and see a stranger coming the other way, most of us drop our eyes and say nothing as we pass. If we stand in an elevator with a fellow rider, most of us back into the farthest corner in steely silence avoiding touch, conversation and eye contact. At the check-out in the grocery store, most of us don't even acknowledge or thank the cashier who is helping us, let alone smile. Babies and small children haven't learned our cultural taboos or adult self-consciousness. Every week at church they make instant friends with the family sitting behind them by sharing their soggy treats, sticky books and toothless smiles. They wave at people in the grocery store and shout things like, "Hey, you want to see my new underwear?"

Once I was holding my young daughter's hand while we passed an ill-kept homeless man on the street. He had long greasy hair, dirty clothes, and smelled of body odor, liquor and tobacco. I lowered my eyes and kept my distance, hoping he wouldn't ask me for a handout. My young daughter, on the other hand, stopped and stood perfectly still, then stared reverently at this man in wide-eye awe.

"Look Mom! It's Jesus!" she shouted excitedly.

The homeless man gently tilted his head in acknowledgement and smiled back at my little girl. Then he glanced up at me with a glimmer in his eyes. We were both humbled at the reverent way my daughter had seen him. When do we stop seeing the amazing beauty in the people around us? When do we stop being excited about our new underwear? When do we stop calling our friends on the telephone to ask if they can come out and play?

Another great truth my children have taught me is to feel what I'm feeling at the moment—to show my vulnerabilities and to hug and kiss a lot, especially at times of parting. For instance, when my son John started kindergarten I took him to his new school several times before the first day and let him try out the playground, meet his teacher and get familiar with the classroom. He knew where to hang his backpack and where to find the boy's restroom. I followed John's bus on the first day and went inside with him for a few moments to participate in a few fun activities the teacher had wisely planned. But when all the parents had to go, the look on John's face was a maternal heartbreaker. When it came time for John to go to school the next day, he was so nervous he paced in circles around me on the kitchen floor while I made his lunch.

"What's the matter, John?" I asked. "Worried about going to school today?"

"Yes," he answered with his eyebrows lowered.

"What are you worried about John?" I asked.

John tried to hold back tears by rubbing his eyes with his fists before he blurted, "Mostly, Mom, I'm just missing you."

"Would it help if I kissed your hand? Then every time you starting missing me you could put your hand on your cheek and I'd be there kissing you?"

John thought for a long while, and then seriously replied, "No.

That won't work."

So I tried again, "Remember when your sister Aubrey had to leave to go to school in Pennsylvania and she was a little scared and sad but she went anyway?" I asked. John nodded. "Remember when Aubrey said that when she gets lonely or sad, she thinks about something happy? What if I put a sucker in your backpack and every time you feel lonely or sad, you start thinking about that sucker?"

John thought for a long while then seriously answered, "I don't know. I'm not sure that will help, Mom."

"What if I give you a hundred hugs and kisses before you go? Do you think that would work?" I asked again.

John didn't have to think. He responded immediately, "Yes. That would definitely help, Mom."

I found a sucker and tucked it away in a secret pocket of his backpack and then we started the hugging and kissing. John carefully counted until we reached a hundred. The steps on a school bus are like scaling Mount Everest to a small five-year-old. Yet when the time came, John hesitantly braved the heights and found his seat on the bus without me. I waved and blew him kisses while he drove away.

Because John was my ninth child to start school, I knew how precious and fleeting childhood is. I also knew how much courage it takes to be a child, to welcome a child into your life and then let that child go. I want to be like my children when I grow up. Children can teach us so much more than we can teach them. I believe we will find our way back to God if we allow children to be our guides.

PUT IT INTO PRACTICE

PRACTICE: Build a snowman, sand castle or fort.

PRACTICE: Touch a prickly caterpillar, frozen icicle or warm wet sand.

PRACTICE: Smell bread fresh from the oven, air after a rain storm or a newborn's skin.

PRACTICE: Eat dessert first.

PRACTICE: Hug tight around the neck and give nose kisses.

PRACTICE: Read children's books out loud.

PRACTICE: Splash in the bathtub or camp out in the back yard.

PRACTICE: Draw a picture and give it to your best friend.

PRACTICE: Wave, smile and talk to strangers. Ask hundreds of questions.

PRACTICE: Frame a picture of yourself as a child and put it where you can see it everyday.

Celebrating Life

"The Lord is my shepherd;
I shall not want."

Psalm 23:1

Secret # 14

Celebrate each day as a gift.

After replacing negative thoughts, calling on God, changing our attitude, feeling gratitude, deepening our perspective, becoming an inverse paranoid, muddling along, funeral thinking, healthy adjustment patterns, smiling, sharing mistakes, doing new things and becoming more childlike, we have reached a place in our journey when we now have the wisdom to celebrate each day as a precious gift.

Several years ago my oldest daughter went in for her ultrasound to determine the health and sex of her unborn baby. I waited for her to phone that evening. When I answered her call I could immediately tell something was wrong.

"It's a boy," my daughter April said. "But Momma, they can't find his brain."

At first, we prayed for a miracle. Then we learned that sometimes miracles hide. Caleb was born on a bright, wintry morning that just happened to be my birthday. He couldn't breathe or eat on his own and was immediately assisted with tubes and monitors. It was an emotional roller-coaster ride those first few days with doctors and nurses all preparing us for the worst. Finally they told us there was nothing more they could do for him and advised my daughter and son-in-law to take him home and let him die surrounded by a loving family. They declared Caleb "not compatible with life," and "not viable."

My daughter and her husband apprehensively brought their fragile son home, still resiliently clinging to life. The hospital staff called ahead and set Caleb up with hospice because they had no hope he would live more than a few hours or days. They advised us to buy a burial plot and continually warned us of his imminent death. Finally my daughter and I looked at each other and said, "We're not listening to those people any more." So what did we do? We made a choice. We decided we could spend Caleb's entire life anxious and scared he might die at any moment, or we could celebrate each day we were blessed to have him with us.

Before long Caleb was breathing on his own and continues to bless our lives. In the beginning, my daughter celebrated his birth every week instead of every year with balloons and cupcakes until we gained ten pounds. So we stopped the cupcakes but the celebrating goes on. We prayed for a miracle and we got one—Caleb's birth, mission and the sacred impact he has on those around him— his spirit, eternal identity and most of all the loving, individual relationship he has with each of us. Those are true miracles. Caleb has taught us all human life has a divine purpose and is precious and holy.

God often wraps blessings in disguise. Tender mercies come to each of us if we will receive God's love amidst the complexities of living. God's love is always there. We just need to open the windows to our hearts. Like morning's earliest light, God's love is the soft illumination dissipating the dark night, gradually flooding our hearts with full, excellent brightness. None of us knows when our time in this life will end. We can live in constant anxiety or choose gratitude and holy blessedness for every glorious day.

Celebrating life doesn't have to be all bells and whistles. Some of the best celebrations are savoring the common or ordinary moments of each day. For instance, celebrating life may be as simple as establishing a meaningful dinner hour. We can create daily gatherings where each person in our household talks, enjoys delicious food and is fed by our love. We establish a dinner hour as a soul-nurturing experience for every member of the family even if we live alone.

Another way to celebrate life is to become more aware of the value of our precious time. Contrary to the world of money where some have little and some have a lot, we're all given the same amount of time in an hour, day or week. The only variable is that we don't know how much time we have before we die. So time is limited. It is not possible for any of us to be so rich in time that we can buy everything. So there are vital choices to be made, every moment of every day.

One helpful way to look at life is to view living as a shopping spree to the ultimate store. This store has everything for sale. We can buy a mansion in the best neighborhood, expertise on a musical instrument or a loving relationship with our children or spouse. We are required to choose each day. Should I read a book to my child or close one more deal at the office? Should I take a walk with my spouse or go to a planning meeting? Spending time on people is always a wise investment. Someday we will all look back on our lives and evaluate how we've spent our time and whether it was a wise investment. The problem is we don't have the ability to go back and invest differently. Our mistakes or deposits have been compounding.

So it is important to make daily deposits versus withdrawals in relationship accounts. The best investment advisor is and will always be our hearts. When we listen to our hearts and spend our time accordingly, we will always have a good return on our investment.

In our family we have a secret code for encouraging each other when one of us has to do something hard or perform. When one of us in up on the stand or the stage and the rest of us are in the audience, we wink. Winking means, "You can do it. You're wonderful. I love you." Caleb definitely knew the family code. He was born with one eye missing, one eyelid permanently closed. So he's always winking at us, always saying, "You can do it. You're wonderful. I love you."

On the days when you feel like throwing yourself a pity party—don't. Nobody will show up but you and nobody will bring balloons or cupcakes. Then remember Caleb and contemplate how lucky you are to see, hear, touch, eat, move, feel, taste and talk. Just being alive is such a delight. Celebrate the simple pleasures. Take nothing for granted. Every moment is a gift, each breath a miracle.

PUT IT INTO PRACTICE

PRACTICE: Plan a nontraditional celebration such as "Happy Tuesday!"

PRACTICE: Have an occasional, do-nothing day when you are simply kind to yourself.

PRACTICE: Take a bubble bath while sipping on a tall, cool drink.

PRACTICE: Spend a day at the beach, mountains or desert. Then go for a creep instead of a hike. Notice all the small miracles you usually miss.

PRACTICE: Use your best dishes, linens and towels for everyday. Wear your fancy clothes at home simply because you feel like looking fancy.

PRACTICE: Arrange a bouquet of fresh cut flowers for the kitchen table.

PRACTICE: Truly keep the Sabbath with these R's: rest, renew, rejoice, remember, and seek revelation.

PRACTICE: Leave space for quiet contemplation each day. Don't over-schedule yourself.

PRACTICE: Take walks alone. Let Mother Nature nurture you.

PRACTICE: Create renewing traditions of celebration unique to you and your family for times of birth, graduations, marriages and death.

Loving Someone

"Love thy neighbor
as thyself."

Matthew 22:39

$\mathcal{S}ecret~\#15$

Love someone.

After replacing negative thoughts, calling on God, changing our attitude, feeling grateful, broadening our perspective, becoming an inverse paranoid, muddling, funeral thinking, developing healthy adjustment patterns, smiling, sharing mistakes, doing new things, becoming more childlike and celebrating life we are able to have the richest of all experiences in life—loving someone.

Love is a profound commitment and thoughtful decision to actively assist someone's spiritual growth and progress toward God. There is no commitment in this whole world quite like loving someone. Love is a journey unlike any other; for when we truly love someone, we give them both roots and wings. We understand when we need to hold on and when to let go—and that's not easy.

A while back my son Jordan packed up all his childhood possessions. He took his basketball card collection, his favorite books, clothes and stereo. Jordan and his new bride were moving into their first apartment. After this brand-new family of two finished packing the truck and waved goodbye, I walked down to my son's empty room and noticed a pillow he'd left on his bed. Now mind you, this was not just any ordinary pillow. Years ago I pieced a quilt for Jordan's Christmas present using his old blue jeans. I backed this memory quilt with red and blue checked flannel and made a window valance to match. With the last small scrap, I made a small throw pillow for Jordan's bed.

When I saw that small red pillow, it immediately took me back to the morning when I was standing in Jordan's bedroom as he finished packing for his two-year foreign mission to Germany. That's when I noticed he'd packed that red-checked pillow. I knew he had very limited space in the luggage because he was going overseas.

"Sure you want to take this?" I asked as I pulled the pillow from the suitcase.

My son grabbed the pillow from me and answered firmly, "yes." This is not just any ordinary pillow, Mom. You made this pillow for me and I've grown up hugging it when I go to sleep every night." Then he carefully replaced the pillow in his luggage. So when I went to Jordan's room after he'd left with his new wife for his new life, there was that same red pillow on the bed, left behind this time. I realized he wouldn't need it any more. He'd have something much better to hug at night now. Yet when I saw that old, red pillow, something inside opened up and the flood gates broke.

"Stop crying, Mommy," my four-year-old said as he walked into the room. "You're making me nervous. Don't worry, Jordan will come home and visit sometimes."

"I know," I answered taking my young son in my arms and hugging him a little more tenderly. "I'm so glad you're here with me for a while."

Yet even then I knew it would not be much of a while. For I have come to know from personal experience that children grow up. As a mother I know it would be unloving to hold my child back from growing up and taking flight. Yet I firmly believe I've earned the right to sit on the bed and cry for as long as I want after they leave. Then before we know it, the tables turn and children are holding our hands.

When my mother-in-law died, a circle of children surrounded her bed at the hospital, holding her hands before she left us and went ahead to a place we could not go.

"You've been the best mother in the world," we children echoed each other around her hospital bed as she took her last breaths. "You did a great job. We love you, Mom. You can do it. It's okay if you have to go now. We'll miss you but we'll be all right. Don't worry about us. Goodbye, Mom."

Loving someone means holding on and letting go every single day. When we just can't stand it any more, we can offer a prayer and feel the presence of someone who loves us enough to let us go. It doesn't make it any easier, but if we allow ourselves to feel everything, the joy and the pain, the love and the loss—we will know that when we left heaven long ago, someone cared, someone wept, someone loves us, someone is missing us and hoping we'll come back home some day.

I used to wonder why older couples were always telling me to enjoy my children while they were home because before long they'd be gone. I thought those people were senile and just forgot all the hard parts. I knew being a mother was exhausting and figured old people could afford to be sentimental because they didn't have to deal with the day to day mess and stress of life with small children any more. It didn't occur to me that those wiser parents had already experienced what I was going through and actually missed it when it was over.

When we're young parents and can't see the end from the beginning, the ability to have children is often taken so casually. We have no idea that loving or not loving this child will affect thousands of people for generations. We don't understand what we've been given. Mostly we see what we seem to be giving up. Yet, as the years go by, we realize that our opportunity to love a child is God's greatest gift to us. Once I read about the last hours of a famous author. On his deathbed a reporter asked him if he was content surrounded by all the prize-winning books he'd written. The author turned to the reporter and replied that if he had it to do over again, each one of those books would be a dearly loved child and grandchild.

If we choose to love someone, will our love always be returned? No. Feeling the pain of not being loved but choosing to love any way, breaks our heart. As we go to our creator with a broken heart, God's enduring eternal love will more than compensate. As we are filled with God's love, there is nothing left to fear. Endowed with

God's love we can better endure pain, freely forgive and renew our strength.

We don't have to be disillusioned when we don't get the love we want from others. We need only concern ourselves with the quality of love we offer. Too often we find ourselves holding back love, afraid of being hurt—giving only to get—sharing love only when we feel love coming back. Our hearts will keep getting smaller and the world will keep getting colder when we live that way. If we depend on other humans, we will always be disappointed and disillusioned. When we focus on receiving God's love for us, we experience what real love feels like so we can offer it to others. We concern ourselves more with the quality of love we give instead of the love we receive. The love we offer others is the most important work we will ever do. People are the only things worth living and dying for. Love is the only thing that lasts—it really is.

Love won't fail us as long as we give it. When we choose to love, we live in a warm inner world of appreciation, gratitude and affection. There is nothing more important to do with our lives than love someone. Ultimately every sacrifice we make for another human being contains our life's greatest meaning—every choice to love, our life's greatest purpose.

PUT IT INTO PRACTICE

PRACTICE: Select someone and practice loving them for the rest of your life.

PRACTICE: Surprise someone with a love attack, complete with balloons, flowers, candy, etc. Fill their face with kisses and their arms with hugs.

PRACTICE: Make a new friend. Call them up and ask them to come over to your house and play with you.

PRACTICE: Practice being tuned in to those you love: turn off your cell-phone, make eye-contact and listen with your attention and all your heart.

PRACTICE: Perform common chores and work with love: make your bed with love, prepare supper with love and wash the dishes with love. There is a higher purpose to everything we do if we are aware and experience the sacred in the ordinary.

PRACTICE: Cradle someone you love in your arms no matter how big they are.

PRACTICE: Let love sparkle through your soul and out your smiling eyes and lips.

PRACTICE: Create a sense of welcome in your heart and home.

PRACTICE: Feel good about who you are and how far you've come. Discover and offer your unique gifts. Share a kind word or offer a helping hand to someone in need.

PRACTICE: Slow dance with someone you love in the kitchen.

About the Author

Janene Wolsey Baadsgaard is the author of many books and numerous newspaper columns and features as well as magazine articles about family life. She has also taught writing and literature classes at Utah Valley State College. She and her husband Ross are the parents of ten children.